BIBLICAL HEROES

STORIES OF FAITH AND COURAGE

MARK HART

ASCENSION

West Chester, Pennsylvania

Scripture quotations are from the Revised Standard Version of the Bible–Second Catholic Edition (Ignatius Edition) © 2006 National Council of the Churches of Christ in the United States of America. Used by permission. All rights reserved.

Ascension
PO Box 1990
West Chester, PA 19380
1-800-376-0520
ascensionpress.com

Cover design and illustrations by Chris Lewis
Interior design by Ashley Dias

Printed in the United States of America
24 25 26 27 28 5 4 3 2 1

ISBN 978-1-954882-76-8 (trade book)

DEDICATION

· · · · · · · · · · · · · · · · · · · ·

To Maddie, Sarah, and Ruby,
I am honored to be your "second Dad,"
sponsor, and godfather.
I am even more honored to call myself your friend.
You have each grown into incredible,
holy, and virtuous young women,
and I am so thankful your parents brought you
into this world and into our family's lives.
Keep your eyes fixed on him.
Pour into his Word.
Seek him in the Eucharist.
He will never let you down,
abandon you, or lead you astray.
God loves you … and so do I.

CONTENTS

· · · · · · · · · · · · · · · · · · · ·

INTRODUCTION

· · · · · · · · · · · · · · · · · · ·

There are a lot of ways that you can get to know someone. You can hear about them from other people, you
can check out their Instagram stories or TikTok feed, or
you can watch them from afar and see how they interact
with others. If they're famous, you might even catch an
interview online or read a book about their life. None of
these methods, though, are nearly as effective as sitting
with that person, one on one, and asking them meaningful questions like these:

- How does it make you feel when ... ?
- Where did you grow up and what was your child-
  hood like?
- What are you most afraid of?
- When do you feel the most joy?
- Why do you do what you do?
- Who is your personal hero?
- What roles do God and faith play in your life?

Questions like these help you to get past the shallow things we usually talk about so you can really know a person. They reveal a person's true identity. While you can use these questions to get to know other people, they are also a great starting point for getting to know yourself. Where does your identity come from? Where do your beliefs come from? What (or who) do you base your decisions on? These are all important questions to reflect on, and they should all lead you back to one fundamental truth: God is the author of your life.

That's right, God is the author and you are the character in his story, not the other way around. God created you. He loves you and wants you here. God has a plan for you. And if you really want to know yourself, the best and fastest way to do that is to get to know the One who created you.

The Bible is a great place to get to know the Author of your story. By reading about his interactions with other characters, specifically young Bible characters, you can get to know not only how God thinks and moves, but also how others have responded to him in both right and wrong ways. The biblical characters we meet in this book are not fictional like the characters in some stories you may read in English class. These are true stories of faith and courage about real people.

When you read Scripture, you will see that while customs and traditions change, people really don't change all that much. You'll realize that you have more in common with these biblical heroes than you would have originally thought. We aren't just reading about people from thousands of years ago. No, when we read the Bible, it's like we're reading about ourselves. God doesn't change. So knowing what did and did not please God in other people is a great way of knowing what does and does not please God in us.

In this book you are going to be introduced to thirteen young Bible characters and their stories. Some you might know well. Others you might not recognize at all. Some are heroic. And some of the stories are heartbreaking. But they're all thoroughly human. If you look hard enough, you might find a little bit of yourself in each story. At the very least, you'll be introduced to a God who is madly in love with you.

It's important to remember that while God might not love everything you do, he does love you. And he is cheering you on to sainthood. Reading this book will act as a small step in that direction. Some of these characters' lives will make you feel quite holy. Others will teach you how to become even holier. In the pages that follow, you'll be guided and invited to open the Bible for yourself and read parts of their stories again.

These people all have something worth imitating and something worth following. Learn from them. What you'll soon realize is that living as a Christian is not so much about "finding yourself" as it is about finding and unleashing Christ's presence and power within yourself. The more you recognize God's presence in you, your home, your school, the Church, and the world, the better you'll be able to share God's love with all you come into contact with, which is an important part of living as a Christian.

The secret to a joyful life and a hope-filled future isn't about figuring out tomorrow, it's about listening to God today. It's not about being "perfect," it's about letting God meet you right where you are and allowing him to help you grow in holiness one day at a time. God, the Author of Life, has something to say to you through these young biblical heroes who came before you. If you want to know God better, just take a deep breath and turn the page.

It's story time.

CHAPTER 1

· · · · · · · · · · · · · · · · · · · ·

Abel: The Bible's First "Little Brother"

No family is perfect. The Holy Family, consisting of our Lord Jesus, our Blessed Mother Mary, and St. Joseph, is as close as you get.

Every other family is imperfect. Some families are holy, and some are not. Some families are huge, while others are small. Some families are financially well off, and others struggle to pay the bills. Every family is unique in its struggles and in its blessings. Yet, all families have one thing in common: every family, absolutely every family, is imperfect. Those families you see on television, in magazine ads, or on billboards all appear to be perfect in every way. But you guessed it, they're imperfect, too.

Now, some families are a little easier to grow up in than others, but every family has its challenges. I'll use my family as an example. I come from a family of six kids. On the surface it sounds great. There were always people around. The house was busy and loud, and holidays were crazy, noisy, and unpredictable.

I was child number five. The four children ahead of me were perfect, or at least they seemed that way to me. They aced every class they took, and they were the captains of their respective sports teams. In everything they did, they were the best. It wasn't enough that they played an instrument, they had to sit first chair in band. It wasn't enough that they'd get a part in the play, they always had to get the lead part in the play. You get the idea.

As if that wasn't enough pressure, along came one more child after me, my baby brother. He stole all the attention and had absolute parental protection. Everything he did was cute and amazing in everyone's eyes. Suddenly, I felt like nothing I did was good enough. When measured up to my siblings' accomplishments, I felt like a nobody. I became bitter and annoyed. What made everyone else so special?

I felt a lot like the famous biblical character named Cain, who comes onto the scene very early in Scripture.

Cain means "spear."

Cain was Adam and Eve's first son, born after they were thrown out of Eden. He was the only son until, one day, he had a "perfect" younger brother of his own.

Whether you're an older sibling, a younger sibling,

or an only child, the story of the sibling rivalry between Cain and Abel has elements that we can all relate to, and it would be

Abel means "breath."

great for you to take a minute, now, and read the story yourself: Genesis 4:1–12.

> **READ IT: Genesis 4:1–12**

GIVE WHAT'S "RIGHT," NOT WHAT'S LEFT

Cain and Abel's story is famous in Scripture. Did it leave you confused? It's pretty short and, if you don't know what to look for, you might have missed why it was such a big deal to God.

It starts out simple enough, right? Adam and Eve have two sons, Cain and Abel. Together, it's as though the family works on a farm: Cain tends to the crops while Abel tends to the animals. At this point, they decide to make a sacrifice to God.

Cain and Abel both offer a sacrifice to God, but God's reaction isn't the same to each brother. However, a clue is hidden in verses four and five as to why God likes Abel's sacrifice so much more than his older brother's. Take another look:

" ... and Abel brought some of the firstlings of his flock and of their fat portions. And the LORD had regard for Abel and his offering, but for Cain and his offering he had no regard. So Cain was very angry ... " (Genesis 4:4–5)

Many people read over this passage and think that it only has to do with the sacrifice. You see, Abel gave God the best animals that he had. The word "firstling" means the first crop or first animal of a season, which also means the best crop or best animal of that season. The Scripture verse does not make a distinction like that about Cain's fruit offering. It's as if Abel went out into his herd of animals and found the absolute best to sacrifice, but Cain just grabbed whatever fruit was lying around (possibly bruised or rotting) and let that be his sacrifice. Imagine how good Abel's sacrifice must have been to be pointed out like that. I mean, that must have been some really good meat to make God so pleased, huh? It must have been the biggest, fattest, juiciest Grade A steak this world has ever seen for God to be so wowed by Abel's sacrifice, right?

Genesis comes from a Greek word that means "beginning."

Well, not exactly.

Yes, it does say that the offering was Abel's best, the

prime choice, but what pleased God wasn't so much Abel's animals, but Abel's attitude. Notice that the verse says, "But for Cain and his offering he [God] had no regard." So it wasn't necessarily the crop that God was displeased with. God was displeased with Cain; something was wrong with Cain's attitude or with Cain's heart.

God even gives Cain another chance, explaining that if he offered a better sacrifice, he, too, would be held in high regard (Genesis 4:7). Before we move on, though, it's important to note something here. God's love for Cain was not based on his performance. God's love is not about "what you do"; he loves you for who you are. Cain's lackluster sacrifice didn't mean that God loved Cain less, it meant that God was disappointed because Cain didn't love God more. He wanted to help Cain understand what true love requires; true love requires sacrifice. When we sacrifice, we show our love by putting others before ourselves.

You read how the story turned out. Cain was so jealous that he lashed out against his brother. He allowed his jealousy and anger to explode. Cain didn't just ignore Abel or punch him or break Eve's favorite vase and blame it on him. No, Cain killed his brother, and God was furious. Cain was then sent off alone. He got what he wanted. He wanted to put himself first and not have to "keep up" with his younger brother anymore. So, there Cain went, alone, ashamed, and awfully miserable.

But wait, this is supposed to be a chapter about Abel, right? So let's take a look at the hero and victim of the story—the Bible's first "little brother," Abel.

FINDING YOURSELF IN ABEL'S STORY

- Have you ever felt "competitive" with a brother or sister?
- Do you hold anything back from God, or do you give him your best, every day?
- Do you worry more about what others think, or what God thinks?
- Have you ever wondered why we "sacrifice" things to God, anyway? Have you ever asked why God wanted us to sacrifice to him? What do you think?

    A. Are animals bad or something?
    B. Should we all be strict vegetarians?
    C. Or is it something bigger?

The answer is C: something bigger. Since God is the Creator of all things, it means that absolutely everything is a gift from the Creator: every drop of rain, blade of grass, piece of fruit, animal, and person.

God does not need us to sacrifice animals for his benefit. God doesn't need food. He asks us because we need it. We, as his creation, need to remember *who* our blessings come from. We need to show the Creator that we love him more than his creation. By sacrificing things back to him, we not only show our reliance on God, but we show him that we are more in love with the One who gives us the blessings than we are with the blessings themselves.

Consider Christmas morning in your home. If you loved the gifts you opened more than the person who gave them to you, you'd be like Cain. If you would rather go without gifts than you would without your parents, you're more like Abel.

The truth is that we make this choice all the time: the choice between ourselves and what we want, and God and what he wants for us. When we pray, it should come from our heart because we want to grow closer to God, not because we want to "get stuff" from him. Sure, we are supposed to go to Mass every Sunday. After all, it's a sin to miss. But we should also go because we have a desire to be there, to worship God and to praise him, to hear his words and receive his Body and Blood.

It's important to note, too, that Abel didn't give his best to God because he wanted to show up his brother. Abel didn't offer his sacrifice to gain the admiration of others or to have a great reputation. Abel gave God his best because he loved God. The same should be true for you and me. We shouldn't sing because we want our voices to sound the best. We should sing because we are truly praising God. We shouldn't go to church because we want others to think we are holy. We should go because we want to grow closer to Christ. In the end, it really doesn't matter what anyone thinks of us, only what God thinks. Abel's sacrifice looked good to the world, yes, but even more meaningful to God was the motivation in Abel's heart. What's on the inside matters far more to God than what is on the outside (see 1 Samuel 16:7).

There is nothing you can do to make God love you more. And there is nothing you can do to make God love you less. He loves you perfectly. Going to church doesn't make God love you more. Rather, going to church helps us to love God and our brothers and sisters in Christ more. Praising God doesn't make God love you more. Rather, praising God helps us to focus less on ourselves and more on God. Serving the poor, giving money to the Church (tithing), resisting temptation and sin, fasting, or making other sacrifices doesn't make God love you more. But it does please him since all of those things help us to grow in love and become more like Christ.

I've met plenty of people in my lifetime who loved God too little. I've never met anyone who loved God too much. Even if you are younger, you can always lead others by your holy example. Don't let being a "younger" brother or sister get in the way of leading your family closer to Christ. Don't let being an "older" sibling get in the way, either. You can always love better. You are able to be more like Abel.

CHAPTER 2

. . . .

Isaac: The Bible's First Father-Son Road Trip

God has a sense of humor. It's a fact. Scripture says, "He who sits in the heavens laughs" (Psalm 2:4). How can you look at an ostrich or a platypus and not at least smile? It takes a creative God, with a great sense of humor, to come up with a giraffe. The fact that we laugh is proof that God laughs, since we are made in his image and likeness (see Genesis 1:26–27).

Now, that doesn't mean that there isn't also a time to be serious. Usually, the reason we think God lacks a sense of humor is because we're told to be quiet and respectful in his house. Obviously, we shouldn't be fooling around or irreverent (showing a lack of respect) in church. At the same time, God rejoices when our laughter is holy and reverent (respectful). The point is that there is an appropriate time for everything. There is "a time to laugh" just like there is "a time to weep" (Ecclesiastes 3:4).

I was about ten years old when I learned this lesson, and I learned it the hard way. My father was working with his tools in the garage. He was swinging a hammer when he missed the nail and struck his thumb. He dropped the tool and started jumping up and down as he grabbed his hand in pain. Not thinking he was too hurt, I sarcastically said, "You're supposed to hit the nail, Dad." If you are ever in this situation, let me assure you that this is not a time to laugh. To make matters worse, my father angrily replied, "Do I look stupid to you?" So, when I replied, "Yes," my laughter quickly turned to weeping.

There are other times in life, though, that God has a way of turning our weeping into laughter. After my grandfather's funeral, for instance, we gathered at the house and told our favorite stories about Grandpa. We sat and laughed for hours, remembering joyful times and funny things he had done. Tears are one of God's most amazing creations. Tears can show up with laughter and with pain, and sometimes, the laughter and the pain collide.

One mother in the Bible who knew both pain and joy was Sarah. Now, Sarah and her husband, Abraham, were no ordinary couple. They were special. They were chosen to do some amazing things for God. Just because they were chosen by God, however, didn't mean that everything was easy or perfect in their lives. Sarah was not able to have children—that is, until God said it was time.

Sarah was ninety years old when she had her son, Isaac. Yes, you read that correctly. It's not a typo. She was ninety, as in "ten years to 100" ninety. In fact, when God told Abraham that Sarah was going to bear a son, Sarah (who was eavesdropping on the conversation) laughed. That's right, she laughed at God. As a reminder of God's incredible sense of humor and his faithfulness, they named their son Isaac, which means laughter (see Genesis 21:6).

Isaac comes from the Hebrew word *Yīṣḥāq*, which means "laughter."

Sarah's weeping and mourning over being childless was, in an instant, turned into laughter and joy. We can learn a lot from Sarah's response. We must remember, always, that God is faithful. God works in his time.

Isaac's story, though, is far from over. Isaac's life is filled with both laughter and pain, with success and heroism, and with disappointment and treachery. There is one story about Isaac, in particular, that has always had the ability to make me laugh and cry. It's called "The Sacrifice of Isaac." Perhaps you've read the story before.

Whether or not you are familiar with it, take a minute and read it for yourself: Genesis 22:1–13.

READ IT: Genesis 22:1–13

PERFECT TRUST BRINGS PERFECT PEACE

Now, this story might leave you a little confused. You might be asking yourself, "What kind of a father would do such a thing?" or, "What kind of a God would want a father to do such a thing?" Without getting too far offtrack, it's important to understand one thing about ancient history. Things then were not as they are now.

In those days, roughly about 2000 BC, human sacrifice was fairly common. Some cultures believed that sacrificing their children to their (false) gods would ensure great blessings for them. But Abraham would probably have been confused when the Lord asked him to sacrifice Isaac, especially after all those years of childlessness and after having Sarah conceive and give birth at such an old age.

Now that you've read the story, you (like most people) might be amazed at Abraham's faith or shocked and grateful for God's daring rescue through the angel. But what about Isaac? People don't often stop to think about what was running through poor Isaac's head that day.

Many scholars believe that Isaac was at least twelve years old when he went on this journey to Mount Moriah with his father. In Mediterranean culture, when a boy turned twelve, he was considered a young man.

If Isaac was a twelve-year-old boy, fast and full of energy, couldn't he have escaped from his elderly father that day? As Isaac watched his father set up the altar with the wood for the fire upon it, he might have grown suspicious. Then, as he watched his father sharpen a knife with no lamb in sight, Isaac may have grown uneasy.

As he followed his father's instructions, lying down upon the altar and feeling the ropes pull tightly against his cloak, Isaac's heart must have raced before eventually breaking. He may have wondered, "How could my father do this to me?" He may have thought, "Why would God, the God my father loved and trusted, allow this?" Still, Isaac did not run. Isaac did not move. Why not? Was it his love and trust in his father? Was it trust in God?

Jesus was twelve years old when he went missing for three days.

Was it fear? We don't know for sure, but Isaac lay there in obedience. Isaac trusted Abraham, who trusted God. Perfect trust brings perfect peace. This story is not just a celebration of Abraham's obedience and trust in God.

This story is, likewise, a celebration of a son's trust in his father.

The attempted sacrifice of Isaac is a true story. It's also a symbolic story, meaning it not only happened one day in history but also pointed to something that was to come about two thousand years later.

You may have noticed a similarity between this story and the Crucifixion of Jesus. The details of this sacrifice, the sacrifice of the father's only son, are important to note. The son, Isaac, carried the wood for the sacrifice (see Genesis 22:6). The father said a lamb would be provided for sacrifice (see Genesis 22:8). Years later, John the Baptist publicly declared Jesus to be the "Lamb of God" (see John 1:29). The ram that was eventually sacrificed was surrounded by a thicket, a bunch of thorny branches, just like the crown Jesus wore on Good Friday (see John 19:2).

Moriah means "God is my teacher" in Hebrew.

What you might not know is that the "land of Moriah" (see Genesis 22:2) is a small mountain range around Jerusalem that was the site of Christ's sacrifice on the Cross. The same ground that was soaked with Abraham and Isaac's tears of joy and pain would also be soaked with the blood and sweat of our Savior, Jesus, and the tears of our Mother Mary, years later.

FINDING YOURSELF IN ISAAC'S STORY

- Do you struggle in being obedient to your parents?
- Do you love God above all else, even more than your family and friends?
- Do you ever think that God wants you to be unhappy or to suffer?

There is no "Instruction Manual" to being a perfect parent except the Holy Bible. Countless books have been written about parenting, but the truth is that the only way to get close to being a perfect parent is by getting to know the only perfect parent, God himself.

It can be difficult to be obedient to our earthly parents because we see their imperfections. Still, we are called to be obedient to them (of course, as long as that obedience doesn't put us in bad or dangerous positions). Why? Well, because God says so, for starters (see Exodus 20:12 and Ephesians 6:2). Additionally, when we learn how to be obedient to our parents on earth, whom we can see, it helps us learn to be more obedient to our Father in heaven.

For that reason, you ought to pray for two things:

First, you ought to pray, daily, for your parents. Pray that they would know God. Pray that they would serve

God. Most importantly, pray that they would love God first, with all of their hearts. The more they love God, the better they will love you, too.

Second, you ought to pray to be childlike in your faith. Children who trust their parents don't consider a parent's warning or guidance to be stifling. They consider it to be freeing. For example, if my youngest daughter really trusts me when I say, "Don't touch the stove," she won't think I am trying to take away her freedom; she will trust that I'm protecting her. If you are childlike in your faith, the commandments won't seem to be taking away your freedom but will be freeing to you, and will ensure your holiness and happiness for years to come. God's plan wasn't and isn't to "hold you back" but to propel you forward to greater joy!

Your love for your parents should never be conditional. It should not fluctuate based on whether they let you do whatever you want. God entrusted you to your parents for this period of your life. Do everything you can to be like Isaac and trust your parents even when it doesn't seem to make sense. Continue praying to God that he will not only watch over you but also guide them in the process.

On Mount Moriah, we see Abraham and his son Isaac demonstrate obedience. At that same location, Calvary, over two thousand years later, we see the perfect obedience of another Son, Jesus. Make your home another

Moriah, where your obedience and sacrifice are so visible that it truly becomes holy ground. Do chores around the house without being asked, clean your room, do the dishes, and obey your parents with things like screentime and bedtime, and you will grow in holiness and virtue.

CHAPTER 3

· · · · · · · · · · · · · · · · · · · ·

Joseph: The Bible's First Daydreamer

Have you ever woken up from a dream that seemed so realistic, you actually asked yourself, "Did that really happen?" One time, when I was in high school, I had this dream where I asked out a girl in my class, and she said yes. I remembered every part of the conversation. I remembered what time I was going to pick her up and where we planned on going. I remembered what she was wearing and what I said that made her laugh. However, the problem came two days after the dream, when I asked her for her home address. She replied, "Why do you need my home address?" I quickly made up an excuse and escaped in embarrassment.

I learned a valuable lesson that day. When a dream seems too good to be true, a good rule for avoiding embarrassment is to quickly ask, "Was I dreaming?" Of course, sometimes dreams do come true. Years later, that girl became my wife.

You might have big dreams for your life. They might involve money or fame or power. You might have simpler dreams for your life that include a dream job or a dream house. You might have godly dreams for your life, like raising a holy family or serving the Church as a priest, nun, or missionary. What are some dreams you have for your life?

The Bible is filled with dreams. God often used dreams to communicate important news to people at vital times of their lives. For example, God spoke to King Solomon, the wise men, and Jesus' earthly father St. Joseph through dreams. But long before any of these important men existed, there was another Joseph, who was quite the dreamer and dream interpreter. This Joseph you can read about in the book of Genesis. He was the

Numbers 12:6 says, "If there is a prophet among you, I the LORD make myself known to him in a vision, I speak with him in a dream."

eleventh son of Jacob. And even though parents aren't supposed to play favorites, Jacob did. Joseph was his favorite son.

WHEN A DAYDREAM
BECOMES A NIGHTMARE

Joseph's older brothers were, technically, his half brothers. They all shared a father, Jacob, but the first ten boys came from three different mothers. Joseph was the firstborn son of Rachel, who was Jacob's true love. Jacob even made Joseph a special coat, "a long robe with sleeves" (Genesis 37:3). In Scripture, robes are symbolic of importance, wealth, power, and even royalty. This special gift from Joseph's father made his brothers envy and hate him.

> **St. Joseph went to Egypt after a dream, too (taking Mary and Jesus along with him).**

When Joseph was probably sixteen or seventeen years old, his role as the favorite son became too much for his brothers to handle (Genesis 37:2). He had been telling his brothers about a series of dreams he was having. In one dream, for instance, the sun and the moon and eleven stars were bowing down to him. It didn't take long for his family to "interpret" what they thought Joseph was saying. "You expect us to worship you and bow down to you?" they asked through clenched teeth and curled lips.

So, one day, when Joseph joined his brothers in the fields to shepherd the flocks and their parents were nowhere in sight, his brothers hatched a plan to kill him.

Luckily for Joseph, one of the brothers ended up pleading for his life. So, rather than killing Joseph, they threw

The name Joseph means "to increase."

him into a deep hole instead. A little later, when they saw foreign traders passing by on their way to Egypt, they decided to make a profit off their brother and sold Joseph into slavery for twenty pieces of silver. This story makes those little arguments with your siblings seem like nothing, huh?

Take a few minutes, now, to re-read this story right out of your Bible and see what other details jump out at you: Genesis 37:3–34.

READ IT: Genesis 37:3–34

Now, even though Joseph was taken to a foreign land, God was still with him and watched over him. Joseph ended up working for a high-ranking officer in the Pharaoh's courts named Potiphar. Potiphar was impressed with Joseph and over time entrusted him with a lot of responsibility. The problem was that Joseph was a very charming and good-looking guy, and Potiphar's wife also had her eyes on him (Genesis 39:6). She flirted with Joseph, but Joseph was a godly man, filled with integrity and self-control (Genesis 39:7–11). Integrity is a big word that means you have strong morals; integrity is who you really are, whether people are watching or not. Joseph never gave in to her temptations, but Potiphar didn't believe him. So he threw Joseph into jail. Soon after he began his jail sentence, Joseph began interpreting the dreams of his fellow prisoners, and in time, his gift for interpretation paid off.

When the Pharaoh began having nightmares that no one could explain, one of his officers, who had been Joseph's old cellmate, knew just where to look for help. All of a sudden, Joseph was standing before the Pharaoh, being asked to interpret the dreams of the most powerful ruler on earth. Joseph warned that the dreams revealed a famine (a long period with no food) coming to Egypt. His interpretation set a plan in motion to prepare for the famine by storing food for several years prior.

Judas Iscariot betrayed Jesus for 30 pieces of silver.

The Pharaoh was so grateful that he promoted Joseph to the highest rank in the courts. And this all happened by the time Joseph was thirty years old (Genesis 41:46). Joseph's faithfulness to his God and to his own dignity, as in the situation with Potiphar's wife, was rewarded in ways he never imagined.

HARD CHOICES:
REVENGE OR RECONCILIATION?

The story gets even better for Joseph (and his family) in the years that follow. You know that famine that was coming to Egypt, right? Well, it hit Joseph's hometown, too. A few years later, Joseph's brothers journeyed south to Egypt, looking for help and for food. At one point, his older brothers who had wanted to kill him, and later sold him, ended up standing right in front of Joseph, the second most powerful man in Egypt.

Saints Peter and Paul also spent time in prison for loving God (see Acts, 5, 12, and 16).

They didn't recognize their little daydreamer brother, though. They hadn't seen him in about twenty years! And Joseph would have been cleanly shaven with shorter hair, as was the custom in Egyptian culture. Joseph, however, recognized the hungry and filthy bunch in front of him as his brothers, and he was faced with a choice. Joseph had the power to send them away hungry and to get revenge for all that they had done to him. Joseph also had the power to forgive those who had wronged him. Given the kind of young man Joseph has already shown himself to be, you can probably guess which one he chose.

You can read Joseph's story now, and you should. The Bible is a gift from God that you can read yourself to learn more about the Author of your story. It's not just for others to read or proclaim to you. Open its pages and let God "speak" to you in a way that can change your life.

Take some time and read about this powerful reunion between Joseph and his brothers in Genesis 45:1–15 and with his father Jacob (Israel) in Genesis 46:28–47:2.

> **READ IT: Genesis 45:1-15 and 46:28–47:2**

FINDING YOURSELF IN JOSEPH'S STORY

- Have you ever felt betrayed or abandoned by the people you love the most, even your own family?
- Have you ever been tempted to do wrong when no one else was watching?
- Have you ever wanted to get revenge on someone who has wronged you?

Joseph's story might seem too "Hollywood" to be relatable at first. It's a true story, a real story, better than anything you could see on reality television. When you look a little deeper, though, past all of the drama of the murder plot, the sale into slavery, the flirtation and temptation and jail term, the dream interpretation and famine, what you're left with is a story of heroic virtue.

Joseph loved God. Joseph loved his family. Joseph used his gifts to serve others. Joseph had respect for himself, and he had respect for women. Joseph knew God hadn't abandoned him even when everyone else had.

Doing what is right is never easy, but doing what's right is always right. The sufferings that come from sin are painful, long-lasting, and deadly. The suffering that comes from doing right can be painful, but it brings joy and peace and freedom. Like Joseph, when you're feeling abandoned or alone, remember that the Lord made you and that he wants good things for you. He wants to bless you, and he will if you are willing to follow his plan for your life instead of your own.

Joseph wasn't trying to brag when he shared his dreams with his family. The Lord had given Joseph a gift, and he was just sharing that gift with the world. Don't play small with the world. If God has given you a gift, whether it's in music or sports, in writing or speaking, in academics or relationships, use that gift for God's glory and be humble about it.

Joseph's story reminds us, too, that even when things go wrong, God has a way of making them turn out very right if we're patient. Be patient with God. Be patient with your family. Be patient with yourself. While you might not see clearly how the story of your life will end, trust that God's plans for you are far better than anything you could dream up on your own.

CHAPTER 4

. . . .

Miriam: The Bible's First Babysitter

Whenever a new babysitter would come to our home for the first time, my wife and I would put her through about a twenty-minute training session. It was like an army boot camp in the suburbs. We spent time explaining where diapers were kept and where bath supplies were found. We walked the sitter through the kitchen, opened the pantry and refrigerator, and explained who can eat what without getting sick. We took her through the various rooms, pointing out potential safety hazards and laying down the house rules, just in case our children attempted to take advantage while we were out.

As much as I love my children, it was always more difficult for my wife to leave the kids. A mother is always concerned about what might happen to her children when they're out of her eyesight. Twenty minutes down the road, some parents are still worried that a child will choke on a toy or try parachuting off the roof when the sitter isn't watching. The truth, though, is that a responsible babysitter can handle it. A good

To read about Moses' encounter with the burning bush, read Exodus 3.

babysitter knows not to let a child out of her sight. A good babysitter is more worried about the innocent toddler than the incoming text message.

It's easy for babysitters to pay attention when they're paid to do it. When teenagers are babysitting their own siblings, however, and for no money, they don't always pay as close attention. Some older siblings think to themselves, "We're at home. He knows the rules. What could happen?" I mean, how dangerous could your own home be, right? How closely do you really have to watch a little brother in the safety of your own neighborhood?

What if your neighborhood, your entire country even, wasn't safe?

Imagine that your mom just gave birth to your new baby brother. It was a great blessing that came during a really hard time for your family. Money was tight. You lived in a home that was quite poor. Your family was living in a foreign country, and the local government, who despised you because of your ethnicity, barely allowed your family to eat. It was a violent country and time period. You had seen many of your relatives and close family members die from starvation, beatings, and various diseases. To make matters worse, the head of the government just issued a new law, saying that all newborn sons of your race should be taken from their parents and drowned in a river.

This situation might sound insane and unrealistic, but it happened. In fact, this was the setting that Moses was born into. You've heard of Moses. You might remember how God spoke to Moses through a burning bush. You probably recall the story of Moses leading God's people, the Israelites, through the Red Sea. You remember how God gave Moses the two tablets containing the Ten Commandments.

Long before any of these events, Moses was in great danger. The Pharaoh decreed that all sons born to Hebrew women should be taken and thrown into the Nile. Moses' mother acted courageously and swiftly, though. She gave birth to Moses and hid him from the Egyptians for three full months. When she could no longer hide him, she placed him in a basket woven out of branches and floated him down the Nile River. Like any good mother, she couldn't just abandon

To read more about the Red Sea, read Exodus 14.

him, so she asked Moses' older sister, Miriam, to keep an eye on the basket, making her the Bible's first official babysitter (Exodus 2:4).

She walked along the banks of the Nile, following the basket that held her baby brother. Eventually Moses' basket found its way to a shore where the Pharaoh's daughter was taking a bath in the waters. The Pharaoh's daughter saw the baby and, re-

The name "Moses" means "to draw out of the water."

alizing it was a Hebrew child, decided to save his life secretly and raise him as her own son. She brought the baby out of the Nile and found a Hebrew mother to nurse him. The coolest part of the story is that the woman she selected to care for Moses until he was older turned out to be his actual mother! (See Exodus 2:8–10).

At this point in the story, Miriam disappears for a while. When we see her again, years later, God has already called Moses to be a prophet. Moses was told to lead the Israelites out of Egypt, and his brother, Aaron, and sister, Miriam, were to lead right by his side.

SOME BABYSITTERS MAKE A "PROPHET"(ESS)

Prophets hold a very important place in the Bible. In fact, a large chunk of the Bible consists of the writings of the prophets. The prophets were not magicians or fortune tellers. They were ordinary people called to share extraordinary things.

Miriam was the first prophetess listed in Scripture. While we aren't exactly sure what God told her to say, the book of Exodus lists her with this title and great honor (Exodus 15:20). It seems, though, that after some time Miriam might have gotten a "big head" over her role.

Sometime after Moses received the Ten Commandments, while the Israelites were wandering through the desert, Miriam disagreed with the way her younger brother Moses was leading and disliked the way things were going.

Take a few minutes and slowly read the scene for yourself: Numbers 12:1–16.

READ IT: Numbers 12:1–16

Miriam had become very self-focused. "Hasn't the Lord also spoken through us?" she asked. Basically, the older sister was looking at her younger brother and wondering, "What makes him so special?" Miriam's jealousy didn't kill Moses, though, as Cain's had killed Abel. Nor did it enslave her little brother, as Joseph's brothers had done to him. No, Miriam's jealousy only enslaved herself.

God's punishment of leprosy was not as painful as what came with it. Leprosy meant you were no longer part of the community. Lepers at the time had to remove themselves from the rest of the community, so as not to contaminate anyone else with their disease. This punishment was far worse than Miriam's skin becoming white and flaky and contagious.

Miriam was entrusted with much, but she abused the power and trust that both God and the people had placed in her. The minute she started thinking about what she deserved, rather than what God deserved, the people who followed her began to suffer. The physical effects of leprosy were plain to see as Miriam walked on the outskirts of camp for that week. The truest effects of gossip and mistrust, however, are always far deeper. Even

To read more about the Ten Commandments, read Exodus 20.

Miriam's whitened skin could not compare to how much pain she was feeling in her heart, after hearing God ask her why she had turned on Moses, God's "servant" (Numbers 12:7).

God punished her for her own good. God taught Miriam a lesson, as good parents are often forced to do. The leprosy helped Miriam appreciate the importance of community. It taught her humility, and it helped her grow in love, not spite, for her God who had already given her so much.

FINDING YOURSELF IN MIRIAM'S STORY

- Do you ever feel like you don't get the attention that you deserve?
- Do you struggle with wanting others to notice you or listen to you?
- Do you ever gossip about others with the desire that they, or you, be seen differently?

We can learn a lot from Miriam. Miriam was entrusted with a great deal of responsibility. We can learn how important it is to watch out for our little brothers and sisters in our families, and also our little brothers and sisters in the faith. We need to protect them. We need to offer a good example to them.

We can also learn that words have power. If the words we use are designed to build God's Kingdom, he blesses them, and lives are saved. If the words we use tear down the Kingdom by tearing down others, he does not bless them, and eventually, we will be without community.

Usually, when we talk about gossip, we hear about how painful its effects can be on the victim. Gossip has the power to destroy a person. But what about the person or people who are gossiping? Why do so many people do it?

Some people are nosy. Some people are bored. Some people are judgmental, and others are just rude. Most of the time, though, the one thing that gossipers have in common is that deep down, they don't like themselves. Rather than focus their energy on improving themselves, they tear down other people. It makes them feel superi-

To read more about the dangers of gossip, try James 3:5–10, 14.

or when they find faults in others without having to focus on their own. Gossip is one of the greatest tools of the Devil, in his attempts to destroy Christ's Kingdom on earth.

All that being said, it's normal to want to be heard and seen. It's human to desire respect. It's not wrong to want others to see that you are special or that you have something to say. The question is whether you want attention for your own glory or for God's. God can and will use you—even as a prophet—to live and speak in his name, but not for your glory or fame. God wants others to know him and his perfect love. If you want to be heard and noticed and remembered, live for God, which will have people talking about you a whole lot longer. People will remember you for how much you loved him.

As you take a more active role in your Faith, you're going to find yourself in some tough situations from time to time. Sometimes it is better not to say anything at all and just to preach by a holy example. Don't forget the fact that "actions speak louder than words." On the other hand, in certain situations, if you don't speak up because you're uncomfortable, God's truth will go unspoken.

CHAPTER 5

. . . .

Ruth: The Bible's First Employee of the Month

Middle school is tricky. Classes get harder than elementary school. Homework often increases. Friendships often change. Hormones are going crazy. Everyone is growing at different rates and maturing at different levels. Insecurities set in more as you become more self-aware about the changes you and your peers are all going through. It's easy to feel really out of control. Then you add in the pressure of school and grades, and all of a sudden, life can become more stressful than it ever was before.

By the time I got to eighth grade, I was ready to move on to high school. I was tired of the middle school drama. To be honest, though, I was kind of "checked out" for a lot of my eighth-grade year. I wasn't trying as hard in class.

I wasn't studying as hard. I was sort of sleepwalking through the fall, and it all seemed fine until I saw my grades starting to slip. One class in particular became a real problem for me: science. I was good at math and religion and social studies and stuff, but science always messed me up.

It was near the end of the semester, and we had a big final test coming up. I made a commitment to myself, my teacher, and my parents that I was going to study harder. I poured hours into that science book, took notes, memorized the material, quizzed myself. I really felt ready. But despite my hard work and preparation, when the day of the test finally came, it was even harder than I could have imagined. There were words and phrases that I didn't even recognize (and to be honest, that I'm not sure our teacher ever taught us). To make matters worse, I watched as several of my classmates pulled out cheat sheets from pockets and folders and breezed through it. I was furious. Here they were walking up and handing in tests before time was even up, yet I was struggling—in my academic honesty—just to finish it on time. I turned in my test feeling very defeated.

When the final grades were posted, I was left with a B- while my cheating friends all "achieved" As. My rage escalated. I wanted justice. I had worked hard while they had done nothing, and now I was the one left with the low grade?! For a minute, I thought, "Maybe I'll just cheat next time, too." Just as I was beginning to think that way, my teacher pulled me aside after class. She told me she saw how hard I had worked and that it showed on my test and in my answers. She affirmed me and thanked me and encouraged me to keep

The name Ruth actually translates to "compassionate friend."

trying. She told me that I should be proud of myself, that *she* was proud of me, and that God was, too. I had never thought of it that way.

That conversation changed everything. After that, I did keep trying—in all my classes. God noticed my effort, and I realized if that was true, he must have noticed others cheating, too. Over the next semester I wasn't just able to get my science grade up to an A; I pulled off straight As without ever cheating. That one moment in middle school changed my entire approach to schoolwork and made all the difference in high school, college, and beyond.

SACRIFICE PAYS OFF

In the middle of the Old Testament sits one of the shortest books of the Bible, the book of Ruth. It's the story of—yup, you guessed it—Ruth! Even though this book consists of only four chapters, it highlights one of the strongest and most moral young women in the Bible. Ruth was likely in her late teens or early twenties when the story opens. She was a Moabite woman, meaning she came from the land of Moab, not Israel. This also meant she came from a culture of false gods and didn't know or worship the one, true God of Israel.

In the first chapter, we hear about another woman named Naomi. Naomi was an older, married woman with two sons. She was from Bethlehem (a town you've probably heard of), but she and her husband moved to the country of Moab. Sadly, Naomi's husband died, leaving her a widow. Widows often didn't have money or jobs and had to rely on the kindness and charity of others. She still had her two boys, one of whom married Ruth, and things were OK since the sons and daughters-in-law were around to take care of Naomi and support her. As bad luck would have it, though, Naomi's sons both died after a few years, leaving her, Ruth, and the other daughter-in-law all widowed.

The name Naomi means "gentle" or "pleasant."

This is the first great test of character for Ruth. In Old Testament times, if a woman was widowed, the next of kin, like a brother or cousin, would often step up and marry the widow, to care for her and keep her in the family. Unfortunately for Ruth, there wasn't anyone available to do so. Naomi decided to return to her hometown of Bethlehem, but she encouraged Ruth to stay in

Moab, return to her family, and try to remarry so that she'd be OK. It's at this point in the story that we witness Ruth's strength, dedication, and loyalty.

Take a second now and read Ruth 1:15–19.

READ IT: Ruth 1:15–19

Now, on the surface this might not seem like a big deal. Ruth was just being a good friend and good daughter-in-law to Naomi, right? The truth, though, is that this was a very big deal. Ruth had no family in Bethlehem. She didn't have a job. She didn't have money. She didn't even know or worship their God. When she said, "Where you go I will go" and "your God [will be] my God," Ruth demonstrated that she was all in.

As time goes on, we see Ruth's inner strength come out. She was a hard worker, unafraid to roll her sleeves up and get her hands dirty. She was such a hard worker, in fact, that it changed her life for the better. One day as Ruth was working hard in the fields, the wealthy landowner, named Boaz, showed up and took notice. He was amazed by her work ethic and wanted to reward her.

Read Ruth 2:4–7 and then Ruth 2:10–13.

> **READ IT: Ruth 2:4-7 and 2:10-13**

Boaz was so blown away by this young woman working from dawn until dusk without even taking a break that he had to know more about her. When he learned of her decision to love Naomi and stay with her, to leave her home country and to begin following the God of Israel, he saw that Ruth was a woman of conviction and integrity. Their relationship began with mutual respect and admiration ... and ended in marriage and raising a family in a little town called Bethlehem.

Bethlehem literally means "house of bread." Kind of cool when you consider that Jesus, the Bread of Life, would eventually be born there.

GOD SEES EVERYTHING
... EVERYTHING

On the surface, the book of Ruth functions as a short, biblical love story. It's a quick and easy read about a young woman with integrity. To have integrity means to be honest and have strong moral principles. Again, basically, integrity is "who you are whether people are watching or not." Integrity helps you choose what's right instead of what's popular, kind of like me with that science test and my cheating friends. When you choose what is right—especially when it is not easy—you are demonstrating true integrity.

Integrity also reveals your character. Are you a person who says one thing but does another, or do you follow through on your promises? Words matter, but actions matter even more. Your actions follow your beliefs. It's easy to say that you love God, but actions reveal whether you truly do or not. It's simple to say that you want to be a good person, but this desire is ultimately demonstrated in your actions on a daily basis,

The name Boaz means "strength."

in how you carry yourself and treat others.

God is omnipotent, which is a big word for "all-powerful," and omniscient, which means "all-knowing." He sees all. He knows all. The Gospel of Matthew tells us that nothing escapes God's glance and that he even knows the exact number of hairs on your head (Matthew 10:30). When you make sacrifices, big or small, God sees and notices just like my science teacher did. The world might not applaud you for not cheating or for taking out the trash without being asked, but heaven sees, and heaven is applauding.

FINDING YOURSELF IN RUTH'S STORY

- Have you ever been alone and afraid, unsure of what to do next, like Ruth was after the death of her first husband?
- Have you ever taken a risk and tried something new for someone you love?
- When you are asked to do a task at home or at school, do you always give it your best and work as hard as you can, or do you sometimes give it half your effort just to get it over with? Do people notice? Do you think God notices? Do you think God even cares?

While Ruth's story might not relate that much to yours on the surface, it does offer us important insight into the unpredictability of life. Sometimes things aren't going to go your way, and that's OK. Sometimes you will be lost or lonely or scared, and that's OK, too; God's got you. You might have to take risks or try new things, and that can be scary sometimes. Again, do not fear. Nothing escapes God's glance—he sees and he is in control. As much as you might feel the need to control your life and future, remember you are the character, and he is the author. He's writing your story, so don't give in to the temptation to pull the pen out of his hand. Just trust that everything will work out.

Incidentally, everything worked out pretty well for Ruth. She and Boaz were married and gave birth to a son whom they named Obed. They remained in Bethlehem as their family grew. Obed had a son named Jesse and, eventually, a grandson whom we cover in the next chapter ... and his name was David.

CHAPTER 6

. . . .

David: The Bible's First Rock Star

There are few characters in the entire Old Testament who are better or more well-known than David, the slingshot-wielding, giant-killing, (eventual) king of Israel. That said, though, what many don't know is that David was more than a warrior or leader. David was a talented musician who not only played music but also wrote it. He came from a pretty small town called Bethlehem, which might sound familiar. And while he began his "career" as an innocent, beloved young hero to millions, along the way he made some bad decisions that caused him a lot of pain and broken relationships.

Before we get ahead of ourselves, though, let's take a second and see how much you remember about this biblical "rock star." David was one of the most famous leaders in the history of mankind. He was one of the

David means "beloved."

most important figures in the entire Bible. David was also one of the most powerful men ever to walk the earth. Oh, and David was a sinner.

You may know the story of David. You might know that he is an ancestor of Jesus. You might have heard about how he was a shepherd, or how he was the youngest son of a man named Jesse. You might even know that the prophet Samuel anointed David with oil when he was still a very young man, probably a teenager, and that the Spirit of the Lord "came mightily upon David" (1 Samuel 16:13).

You've almost definitely heard about his fight with Goliath, the mightiest warrior of the Philistine army.

Psalm 23 sounds like something a shepherd would write.

David wasn't looking for a fight—he was a shepherd boy. He was just dropping off some lunch to his older brothers, who were in Israel's army. They were the warriors, not David.

Take a minute and read the story on your own: 1 Samuel 17:1–54.

READ IT: 1 Samuel 17:1–54

Things changed for David that day, as you can see. It only took one rock from the teen's slingshot and the fight was over. This was no Ultimate Fighting Challenge. This was no challenge at all. Goliath was cocky, thinking that his strength could outmatch God's. Goliath had a big head ... until David cut it off. God's blessing was upon David, and when God's favor is upon you, there's

David's anointing with oil and reception of the Spirit is a lot like what happens to you at Confirmation.

nothing you cannot do (Luke 1:37, Philippians 4:13).

While that victory was amazing and it began David's long and impressive career as a warrior, he did far more than just fight. David is also credited with writing many of the Psalms in the Bible.

MORE THAN A MUSIC MAN

Songs tell a lot about the songwriter. When you listen to a song, you can tell what the songwriter is thinking or feeling, or what they want you to think they are feeling. There are 150 psalms in the Bible, and many are attributed to King David. They say a lot about the author, David, but even more about the Author of Life, God.

Psalms are songs that praise or call out to God. We hear or sing a psalm in almost every single Catholic Mass; the psalm follows the first reading. You'll notice that the words and cries of some psalms sound very joyful while others sound absolutely miserable. David wrote about the highs and lows of life. David's own life was a series of highs and lows. Just to offer you a few examples:

- His best friend's dad wanted him dead.
- His first wife was embarrassed and ashamed of him.
- He was the mightiest ruler and warrior on earth.
- His army was powerful and his kingdom was far-reaching, but they were constantly under attack.
- He betrayed his loyal servant and had him killed.
- His own son wanted him dead.

These might not be situations you can relate to at your age. These are hopefully not situations you'll ever have to relate to in your own life, at any age. But there is one afternoon in David's life, in particular, that you might be able to relate to very well.

GOD SEES ALL, EVEN WHEN NO ONE ELSE IS LOOKING

The Bible says it was "late one afternoon" when David got off his couch (2 Samuel 11:2). He was alone. His armies were off fighting, but he had remained back at the king's palace. When he walked onto his rooftop, he looked around, and was quickly shocked as he saw something (some*one*): a woman bathing.

It was at this moment that David had a choice.

He could look away to protect her dignity and his own chastity, or he could let his eyes go where they didn't need to go. He could choose holiness or sin. He was standing at the crossroads of temptation. Rather than looking away and choosing the honorable and

You can read about David's life in 1 and 2 Samuel, 1 Kings, and 1 Chronicles.

manly thing to do, David was selfish, and stared at the bathing woman. He allowed his own lust to get the better of him and used his power to send for the woman, and he sinned. The woman's name was Bathsheba. She was the wife of Uriah, an armor-bearer in King David's army. When he learned that Uriah was her husband, David sinned yet again, hatching a plan for Uriah to be killed in battle so that Bathsheba could be his and his alone.

How did this all happen? How did David go from being the "anointed one," the one with whom God was so pleased, to the one who was so selfish, so lustful, and even murderous?

FINDING YOURSELF IN DAVID'S STORY

- Have you ever done something you knew you weren't supposed to do?
- Have you ever looked at something you knew you shouldn't look at or watch?
- Have you ever done something you're ashamed of in an effort to "cover up" something else you'd done?

The internet is an amazing invention. You can find information about almost anything within seconds. Research for a class paper that used to take your parents or grandparents hours, or even weeks, to find in a library, is now available to you within a click or two. There is no shortage of things for you to read, to listen to, or to watch online, but that doesn't mean that everything online will bring you closer to God.

You know as well as anyone—probably even better than your parents or grandparents—how many "dark" things online actually will lead you into shame and sin, instead of leading you to light, joy, and freedom. Maybe you can relate. Maybe you know the temptation of looking where you shouldn't, at things that you shouldn't. This is what sin does: it replaces freedom with slavery, life with death.

You're not alone.

We all sin. We all fall short of God's hopes and expectations for us. We may be tempted at different times and in different ways, but we are all tempted to sin in some way. We have that in common. You're not the only one who is tempted. You're not the only one who sins. Your parents were tempted. Your grandparents were tempted. The pope is tempted. Your parish priest is tempted. Your teachers and your coaches are tempted, too. Adam and Eve were tempted (and you know how that turned out). Even Jesus was tempted, but Jesus didn't sin.

God knew you would be tempted. He also knows that you can resist all temptations with his help. Check out what it says in 1 Corinthians 10:13:

"No temptation has overtaken you that is not common to man. God is faithful, and he will not let you be tempted beyond your strength, but with the temptation will also provide the way of escape, that you may be able to endure it."

Did you notice what God said there? He didn't say you wouldn't be tempted, he said you won't be overcome by it. He says that no temptation

To "repent" means to turn away from sin (darkness) and turn back to God (light).

is beyond your strength because God always provides a way out if you call on him. He is promising you that you can withstand and endure even the hardest temptations. Not because of how strong you are, but because of how strong he is.

Yes, David sinned. David also repented. He was sincerely sorry for what he had done, and he went to the Lord to make it right. If you have sinned, trust in God's mercy. There is no sin too big for God to forgive. The only sin God won't forgive is the sin you don't ask forgiveness for. God

David's prayer of repentance can be found in Psalm 51. You might recognize it from Mass.

doesn't force his mercy on anyone, but he's dying to give you his mercy. That's what the crucifix is: living proof that God is dying for you to know how much he loves you.

Take advantage of the Sacrament of Reconciliation. Be honest with yourself. Be honest with the priest. There you can sit with Jesus Christ, in the person of your parish priest, and ask him for the help you need to defeat temptation and conquer your sins. Allow the grace of the sacrament to give you strength to start over clean and pure.

Only Christ is perfect. Jesus is the one we look to for our example. Jesus is the one we should pattern our lives after. We seek to be like Jesus, not just to be like athletes or celebrities—or even rock stars.

Another thing you can take away from David's story is how God gave him a variety of gifts, and he used them all. He was a warrior and a writer and musician. You, too, can have lots of interests, and develop your gifts and talents. You can be a leader on your sports team as well as the lead in a play. Or at least participate in two totally different activities. Be open to exploring and using all the gifts God has given you, just like David.

CHAPTER 7

. . . .

Josiah: The Bible's First Preteen King

As I lay there coughing and hacking in my bed, I had no one to blame but myself. My throat was so sore I couldn't even swallow water. My head felt like a hot air balloon, and I couldn't breathe through my nose. I had caught the worst cold I'd ever had, and it was all my fault. I got sick because I cared more about what my friends thought than what my mother said.

I was in seventh grade at the time and had been meeting a bunch of friends at the mall to see a movie. Afraid that they would see me get out of my mother's minivan, I asked her to drop me off about a mile down the street from the entrance. The forecast called for rain, but I didn't care. There could have been a volcano erupting in the mall parking lot, for all I cared. Not only was I foolish, I was stubborn, too. My mother pleaded with me to let her pull up closer, but I said, "No way." We got into a huge argument over it. I said some hurtful things and let my mother know how embarrassed I was of her. To this day, I regret how I treated her that afternoon. My behavior was the embarrassment, not her.

I was in a T-shirt and shorts as the cold front and the eventual thunderstorm came through. I walked through the rain, getting doused by cars driving through the puddles on the street. I arrived at the movies so soaked that I was shaking. My reputation was intact, but my respiratory system was destroyed. The air conditioning was on in the theater, making matters even worse. And during moments of silence in the movie, if you listened closely enough, you actually could hear the water dripping off my shorts onto the popcorn-covered floor below.

It was the longest movie of my life. The closing credits could not come fast enough. That night I felt the sickness creep in, and as expected, I was miserably sick for the next several days. Even more miserable than the sickness in my body, though, was the sickness I was feeling in my soul. I wasn't really ashamed of my mom, far from it. I loved my mom. I just wasn't mature enough to admit it or show it. In my effort to "be a man," I had acted like a bratty little boy.

Middle school brings natural struggles along with it. Your body is constantly changing. Hormones roll around inside of you like pinballs in a machine plugged into a nuclear accelerator. Everyone grows and changes at a different rate. Some begin a semester four feet tall and end it six feet five inches. Others stay the same height for years. Voices change. Complexions change. Friendships change. Relationships change. Family dynamics often change, too.

Some of the middle school youths I meet have great relationships with their parents. They eat together, hang out together, and consider their parents their heroes. Other middle school youths act just like I did: they're embarrassed, annoyed, angry, outspoken, and disrespectful. In short, they seldom stop to think about how their words or actions affect their family. They focus on the "I" in f-a-m-i-l-y.

If they only knew—like I do now—how blessed they are to even have a family, they might act differently. Now, as a parent, I understand two things: first, I'll never be a perfect parent, but I can be a holy parent; second, my kids will never truly know how much I love them, and I can never tell them enough.

Josiah means "the Lord supports."

Most of the time, when teens or preteens are ashamed of their family or embarrassed by them, it's without a good reason. Just because parents act dorky or don't dress very hip is no reason to be embarrassed by them. If you want to talk about a kid who had a reason to be embarrassed by his family tree, look no further than the Bible's first preteen king, Josiah.

NOT YOUR AVERAGE JO(SIAH)

Josiah became king of Judah when he was only eight years old. Can you imagine that? Imagine being made president of the United States at eight years old. The only catch is that you weren't elected. You were given the role even though your family name was tarnished, and you were already considered a horrible person because of your ancestors. Not the best way to start your term as a leader of a nation, huh?

You see, Josiah's family tree gives an all-new meaning to the term "dysfunctional family." Josiah's grand-

Josiah's life is also found in 2 Kings 22–23.

father, King Manasseh, didn't just believe in false gods, he celebrated them. Manasseh built altars to false gods and worshipped them inside the Lord's temple. Manasseh sacrificed one of his own sons in a fire, practiced witchcraft and other forms of evil arts, murdered innocent people, and led an entire kingdom of followers away from the one, true God (2 Kings 21:1–9).

How's that for a messed-up family tree? Wait, it gets worse.

Following Manasseh, Josiah's father, King Amon, continued in the same horrible footsteps. King Amon also worshipped false gods, just like his father. He, too, abandoned the Lord, and was so evil that eventually his own followers killed him in

Josiah made a public covenant to follow the Lord and his commandments.

his own house. It was at this time that young Josiah was named king, carrying with him all kinds of family baggage. Something really interesting happened, though, when Josiah was only a teenager.

Read it for yourself: 2 Chronicles 34:1–7.

READ IT: 2 Chronicles 34:1-7

Now, did you notice how old Josiah was when he began "to seek the God of David" in verse three? It was in the eighth year of his reign. Josiah was only sixteen years old when he stood up and turned his country upside down.

Josiah's family tree was anything but glorious. Yet rather than letting his father's or his grandfather's sins dictate the path of his life, Josiah went further back into his family tree, until he found someone he could look up to. He found King David, whom we have already discussed. While David was not perfect, he was "a man after [God's] own heart" (1 Samuel 13:14). Josiah needed a hero, a role model, and he found one.

The prophet Jeremiah wrote a lamentation (a sad song or poem) over King Josiah's death (2 Chronicles 35:25).

As a teenager, he tore down the altars to false gods, smashed statues of idols, and restored the Temple for proper worship. He prayed the Scriptures, reinstituted and lived out God's law, honored the sacred feast days, and renewed the covenant. He was a humble, prayerful man. Josiah was holy and bold and turned his whole heart to God. In the process, Josiah saved an entire nation from ruin.

The young king understood three things that many of us forget:

1. The pursuit of true holiness is contagious.
2. Humility is a strong weapon in the hands of God.

3. You cannot let your past or your family's past ruin your present or dictate your future.

Josiah went on to reign for thirty-one years, and when he died, an entire nation mourned his death (2 Chronicles 35:24–25). So heroic and beloved was Josiah that hundreds of years later they were still praising his name.

FINDING YOURSELF IN JOSIAH'S STORY

- How does your family tree compare to Josiah's?
- Do you let your age or lack of knowledge keep you from speaking out for God or living for him more boldly?
- Have you ever allowed past failings to make you doubt your present ability or future holiness?

Regardless of how old you are, or how blessed or messed up your family tree might seem, God desires a great life for you (see John 10:10). You might come from a family or a past with a lot of darkness, sin, or pain. If so, it's even more important that you do what Josiah did: look around for holy lives you can pattern your own after. It doesn't matter how young you are. You can live a holy, saintly life today and every day that you walk with the Lord.

You cannot control many of the circumstances in your life. You cannot control whether your parents go to church, if they pray, or if they teach you about the Faith. You can, however, invite them to go to Mass with you, or to pray with you, or to learn about the Faith with you.

If you are holding any grudges or pain, forgive your family members and friends. If you, like me, have caused any pain to others through your words or actions, seek their forgiveness. Remember, parents may not love you perfectly, but they do love you. At the very least, you can pray for your family daily. If you are fortunate enough to come from a holy family, thank God for it and affirm your family for trying to follow God each day. Look around your parish, your youth group, and your school and find people who are trying to live holy lives, and affirm them, too. Thank them for their example.

Remember that you are never too young to lead others to God through your words, and, more powerfully, through your actions. Your life is the greatest invitation others will ever receive to follow the Lord. And on those dark and stormy days, when the heavens open and the rains fall hard, your example will call others out of the rain, away from sickness and sin and into the warmth and love that only God can offer.

CHAPTER 8

. . . .

Jeremiah: The Bible's First Teen Prophet

When I was in elementary school, my life was forever changed. I'd love to say it was because I had a powerful moment at Sunday Mass or because the Lord spoke to me, revealing his love and his mission for my life. I wish. Nope, my life was changed because my older brothers took me to the movies. One amazing Saturday afternoon, with a tub of popcorn and a huge cup of sugar—I mean soda—in hand, I sat back into the cushy seat, and my eyes were opened to a whole new future of possibilities as the words appeared on the massive screen: "A long time ago in a galaxy far, far away ..."

That was it. That was all it took. For the next two hours, I was introduced to the Star Wars universe and to the greatest film I had ever seen: *Return of the Jedi*. It was exciting and funny, and the characters were incredible.

At that moment in my young life, I realized the career that God had designed for me: to become a Jedi myself. I had no understanding at that age that Jedi were not real, and that as a profession, becoming a Jedi was not a true option. Over the course of the next year, when I learned there was no "Force" and that lightsabers had yet to be invented (still hoping, though), I had to come to grips with the reality that becoming a Jedi was not my vocation and true calling, and that God must have other plans for me.

Now, whether or not you're a Star Wars fan doesn't really matter in the big picture of life. What does matter, however, is that you realize that you, too, are a character in God's story. You are here because God wanted you here. He is the author, and you are the character, and each day you live is another page in your story. Realize that if you are alive, you are here by design and here for a reason. God may not have revealed your vocation or life's purpose yet, but rest assured that he

The name Jeremiah means "God will uplift" or "God will exalt."

does have a plan for your life—an amazing plan—that he designed just for you, to bring him glory and to get you to heaven for all eternity.

Of course, being alive doesn't mean life is easy. Every family is different. Every school is different. Every friend group is different. Every situation is different. What is constant, though, is God's presence and his love, even if you can't quite see him at work in your life yet or hear his voice in your heart.

(YOUNG) MAN ON A MISSION

Jeremiah was born during a really difficult time in biblical history. It was about six hundred years before Jesus would be born, and the kingdom of Judah (which was the southern kingdom of Israel) was in bad shape. Through a series of many faithless kings, the people of Judah had turned their hearts away from

Jeremiah lived around 650–570 BC.

the one true God (our God) and begun worshipping false gods. Their hearts and minds were not united, and they broke their covenant with God.

Remember, in a covenant, God enters into a relationship with us. In a covenant, God gives us all of himself along with his mercy and love and asks us to give him all of ourselves. A covenant—if kept—keeps us in this rightly ordered relationship. When we turn away from God, however, and put our time and energy and heart into the false gods of the world (money, power, greed, selfishness, lust, etc.), we break the covenant, and bad things happen. It's important to realize, though, that when bad things happen it's because of our choices, not because God stopped loving us. Sometimes God has to allow bad things to happen to his children so that, hopefully, we or others in our lives will learn a hard lesson and return to him.

God loves us too much to just let us fall off a spiritual cliff, though, so throughout the Bible we see God sending prophets to try to warn the people and help them change direction, away from sin. When God saw how the people of Judah were sinning and turning away from him, he created a new life with a new mission ... one that began in Jeremiah's mother's womb.

The word *vocation* comes from the Latin *vocare*, meaning "to call."

Take a moment to read Jeremiah 1:4–9.

READ IT: Jeremiah 1:4–9

From a very young age—likely as a teenager—Jeremiah understood his vocation and mission to be a prophet of God. This was no easy task or assignment, however, because Jeremiah was a lot younger than the other prophets, teachers, and leaders of the time. Did you catch what Jeremiah's first excuse to God was in those verses? He basically said to God, "But, I don't know how to speak. I'm just a kid."

God repeated his calling even more forcefully after that. Basically, God was saying, "Don't tell me you're too young, and don't be afraid. I'll be with you and I will give you the words you will need." This point is really important. You have probably heard about prophets before. Sometimes we mistakenly think of them as fortune-tellers—that is, as people who see or predict the future as though it's some carnival trick. It's actually not like that at all. Prophets can only share what God puts on their hearts and lips. Prophets are God's messengers and communicators, and they usually weren't well-liked, because the news they brought to people was oftentimes intimidating and hard to accept.

As Jeremiah grew older into his young adult and adult years, things in Judah went from bad to worse. The older leaders refused to listen to Jeremiah's warnings. They wrote him off as too young, or "holier than thou," or just plain annoying. They didn't want to listen to him because they didn't want to listen to God's truth. They grew angry with him speaking hard truths. As time went on, Jeremiah was proven correct in his prophecies, though, and over time the people's sins and hard-heartedness took their toll. They had broken

The word *prophet* is the Greek translation of the Hebrew word *navi*, meaning "spokesperson."

the covenant; God had to allow them to be taught a lesson. The foreign power of Babylon came into Judah and overtook them. The Babylonians destroyed buildings, put up statues to false gods in the Temple, broke up families, and took people far away into slavery.

At this point, God's people became even more upset ... *with God!* Even though God had warned them repeatedly, through prophets like the young, great Jeremiah, they refused to listen. In their pride they thought they knew better than the God who had created them.

Jeremiah is also credited with writing the Old Testament book of Lamentations.

Now, if you were God, would you give up on the people of Judah, who were now worshipping false gods in the Temple that had been created for you? Would you smirk and punish them in a huge "I told you so" moment?

I probably would have. Good thing for all of us that I'm not God.

THE FUTURE IS BRIGHT?

Even though God's people sinned after repeated prophetic warnings, the book of Jeremiah teaches us a vital lesson for life: you might give up on God, but he never gives up on you. If we repent (admit our wrongdoings, seek forgiveness, and change our ways), God will forgive us and help us get back on the right track. Remember, God's desire is not for our blind obedience but instead for our salvation. God doesn't want a resentful "robot" who follows him mindlessly; he wants a thoughtful son or daughter who walks with him faithfully.

During some of the darkest days in Jeremiah's life and

the kingdom of Judah's existence, God gave Jeremiah a great promise and encouragement to share with his people. Now, read Jeremiah 29:11–13.

READ IT: Jeremiah 29:11–13

Did you catch that? Do you see what God says to his children here, in the middle of their suffering, when they are feeling abandoned and forgotten? He reminds them that their future is bright. God assures them that he has a plan—a master plan that will lead them to happiness—if they just trust him and if they seek him. He promises them that when they pray, "he hears them," and when they seek him, "they will find him"— *but they have to seek him*. How? With their whole heart.

Lamentations comes from the root word "lament," which means "to weep." The book describes the people of Judah's sadness after being invaded and deported to Babylon.

They can't just cry out to him to save them and then not follow through. No, they have to be sincere and humble and give God their heart once again, which is how God would reestablish the covenant with his children. Eventually, God's people would be released from captivity and return to their homes in Jerusalem and southern Israel, and Jeremiah would be proven very, very right. The entire book of Jeremiah is a great reminder of the importance of following God no matter what and of preaching truth even if no one wants to hear it!

FINDING YOURSELF IN JEREMIAH'S STORY

- Have you ever been in a position where you had to tell someone a truth that they didn't really want to hear, and it was difficult for both of you?
- Have you been looked down on because you are "too young" or "only a kid" and "don't know what you're talking about"?
- Are you more into your Faith than other family members or friends and it puts you in awkward situations?
- Has there ever been a time that the future looked sad or hopeless, when you just had to pray and trust God?

Jeremiah is likely the youngest prophet in the Bible. As a young man he was called to be God's mouthpiece to a nation and culture that wanted nothing to do with truth or virtue. At times, he felt alone. At times, he decided that he didn't want to preach God's Word anymore ... that he would just hold it inside instead, but then he just couldn't control himself (Jeremiah 20:9). The Holy Spirit compelled young Jeremiah to be bold and speak the truth even to people who thought he was ignorant or immature.

You might not be the oldest, smartest, or even holiest member of your family, but you matter. It's not about how old you are or how much you know or don't know about the Faith or about life, it's about how much you love God and how devoted you are to living a pure and holy life.

God created you with a specific vocation and mission that only you can fulfill. God gave you gifts and talents that are unique to you, blessings he wants you to share with the world. Learn from young Jeremiah and follow in his holy and heroic footsteps. You may not have the title "prophet," but you can still seek holiness in everything you do and in whatever vocation God calls you to in your life.

Be an example in your home. Be an example in your school. Be an example on your teams or in your activities or at your job (someday). Don't do it for attention; do it strictly for God, and let the world see his goodness through your goodness. You may not be able to save a nation—Jeremiah couldn't, either—but he did help save countless souls who turned back to the Lord. You may be young, but you are also mightier than people may see, because God made you for greatness!

CHAPTER 9

· · · · · · · · · · · · · · · · · · · ·

Daniel: The Bible's First Lion Tamer

Flashes of lightning lit up the darkened room. Thunder clapped and rain fell hard. The lights flickered as the power struggled to stay on. I'd been alone in my house many times before, but this night was different. I was in fifth grade, and my parents were out for the night. All of my older siblings were gone, too. It was just me in our big, empty, increasingly eerie house. To make matters worse, I had decided to watch a horror movie I would not normally have been allowed to watch.

I was probably halfway through the movie when someone began knocking on the front door. We weren't expecting any visitors, and as I peered through the blinds of a side window, I realized I didn't recognize the car parked out front. I couldn't get ahold of my parents or brothers, so I barricaded the front door and moved into the corner of the family room, armed only with a bat I had from Little League. It could have been one of my brothers' friends or someone dropping something off for my father. It even could have been a neighbor I didn't know. But it didn't matter. I was already so spooked by the movie that my imagination got the better of me.

Once the knocking stopped, I wondered where the person had gone but was afraid to look back through the blinds. Then, I became convinced that there was someone in the house (thanks, again, to the movie I was watching). This is where things got crazy and I began to give in to fear. Normal sounds started to freak me out. It didn't matter

The name Daniel means "God is my judge" in Hebrew.

what it was—the air conditioner could turn on or the ice maker in the freezer could drop cubes. Sounds I had heard a million times before now began to make my heart race. I started to panic. I was alone and facing certain death, or so I had convinced myself. My pulse raced. I began to sweat. My mouth was parched. Then, of course, the power went out. It was as if I now was in a bad horror movie. I was steeped in the pitch-black darkness and suddenly felt even more alone, if that was even possible.

It was in that moment that I just started praying harder than I had ever prayed, asking God to protect me.

Minutes later, the front door opened. I had never been so happy to see my older brothers. I tried the best I could to hide my fear and nervousness (and baseball bat), but they figured out what was going on pretty

Babylon was about 900 miles from Jerusalem.

quickly. Like typical older brothers, they gave me a hard time and reminded me I wasn't supposed to watch movies like the one I had been watching. Since that night, every time I see a horror movie, or even a preview for one, I remember my fifth-grade heart racing and the first time I called out to God to protect and save me. I have called out to him for protection probably a million times since then, and it's made all the difference in my life. Knowing God is with us no matter the situations we find ourselves in is an irreplaceable gift.

FAR FROM HOME

Recall the story of the amazing king, Josiah, from chapter seven. His faithfulness preserved and ultimately saved the kingdom of Judah ... for a while. Not long after Josiah's death, the nation rebelled against God once again.

It was a dark time for the Israelites. Yes, they were still God's children, but after years of turning their backs on God, he allowed them to learn a hard lesson. At the time, Babylon was the most powerful kingdom in the world, and they soon invaded Judah. King Nebuchadnezzar, the king of Babylon, however, did not just invade and take land or money. No, he sent his armies in with a specific plan and strategy. The Babylonians looked to the younger members of the Israelites

Like every other culture of the time—except Israel—the Babylonians were "polytheistic," meaning they worshipped multiple (false) gods.

and took the "best and brightest" of the youth as slaves back to Babylon. From among them, the king hand-picked the best-educated, best-looking guys with the most wisdom to live and serve on his royal staff. One of the young men selected for this new assignment was named Daniel, who was likely a teenager, and he's the principal character of an Old Testament book that bears his name.

As a slave, it would have been easy for Daniel to be bitter. He could have become angry toward God for letting Judah fall or for allowing him and his friends to be forced into a foreign land. Daniel also could have been filled with anger and hatred toward King

Nebuchadnezzar and his Babylonian captors for violating his freedom and putting him to work in service of an enemy kingdom. No one would have blamed Daniel for being resentful, but he wasn't. The way that Daniel chose to handle the situation shows what made him so special: his holiness.

Even in captivity and surrounded by the worship of foreign gods, Daniel never stopped praying to or praising his God, the one, true God.

Take a moment now to read Daniel 2:20–23.

READ IT: Daniel 2:20–23

Even in slavery, far from home—and as only a teenager—Daniel kept his heart focused on God and his goodness. He didn't let his heart grow bitter. He didn't turn his back on his religion; instead, he *leaned into it*. His faith in God only grew in challenging moments, and that faith would prove very, very necessary for the life-altering moment Daniel would later face.

Persia conquered the mighty Babylonian empire in about 539 BC.

THE HEART OF A LION

As the years passed, Daniel earned the respect of the king and the jealousy of the king's advisors. Even when Babylon was conquered by the Persian King Cyrus, Daniel was still admired and revered by the new rulers.

St. Paul tells us in 2 Timothy 1:7 that "God did not give us a spirit of timidity but a spirit of power."

Over time, King Cyrus died, and King Darius took over the throne. Daniel's wisdom and character impressed King Darius, but his closest followers were threatened by Daniel's faith and infuriated by his popularity. They hatched a plan and tricked the king into making it illegal to pray to the one, true God, instead of to the false gods of the Persians and Babylonians. If anyone broke this new law, they were to be thrown into a lions' den.

Daniel, being a faithful follower, continued to pray morning, noon, and night to the God of Israel, refusing to turn away from his faith or to let others dictate his worship. Daniel was caught praying to God, and even though King Darius had grown to love and admire Daniel, he would not allow himself to look foolish in front of his people. They even threatened him if he did not act. So the cowardly king signed Daniel's death sentence by thrusting him into the lions' den.

You may have heard this story before but not read it with your own eyes. Stop here to read Daniel 6:13–23.

READ IT: Daniel 6:13–23

Daniel's escape from the den of lions is a great reminder to us that God always has our back. It would have been easy for Daniel to abandon his faith and his God out of fear. The minute they rolled and sealed the stone in front of the den, he could have turned away from God, but he chose not to. He prayed all the more, and God sent an angel to rescue and preserve Daniel from otherwise certain death.

FINDING YOURSELF IN DANIEL'S STORY

Now, it's unlikely you will ever find yourself in a lions' den in the twenty-first century. Let's hope not, at least. The truth, though, is that being in a lions' den is a metaphor for living a life of faith. The lions' den could be your school, where classmates wait for you to do anything wrong so they can pounce and mock you. The lions' den could be your online profile or feed, where people might take shots at things you post. The lions' den might even feel like your circle of friends, where, sadly, the people you're closest to might not love you the way you deserve to be loved as a child of God.

- **When you're feeling alone or scared, do you call out to God?**
- **When you feel like others have turned their backs on you, do you trust that the Lord is still with you?**
- **When a situation seems hopeless, do you give up, or *look up* to heaven?**

That stormy night in fifth grade, I was scared. I was in the dark. I felt alone and in danger—much like Daniel did in that lions' den, I imagine. It was only when I stopped and prayed, asking the Lord to be with me and to protect me, that I finally found peace, or inner courage.

> **True courage is a refusal to be mastered by fear; the word *courage* comes from a Latin word meaning "to act from the heart."**

I don't know your family situation. I don't know what life is like in your friend group or at your school. I don't know what the "lions' den" looks like in your life.

But I do know one thing: no matter how scared or alone you ever *feel*, God has not abandoned you and never will. God will be there with you, right by your side, if you have the trust and courage to call on him.

When you have God on your side, there is nothing to fear. No lion is bigger than the lion tamer.

CHAPTER 10

. . . .

Esther: The Bible's First Beauty Queen

Growing up with older brothers, you have to learn how to "take it." In my house, from the minute I could walk, I was sort of a slave. My brothers were constantly telling me to go and get them things. If I refused (and if my mom wasn't within hearing distance), I would suffer their wrath. Sometimes it was a wet willy, and sometimes it was one of them sitting on my chest and dangling spit over my face. At other times, it was a good old-fashioned punch in the arm. As if the physical torture wasn't enough, there was also the teasing. No matter what I said, they could find a way to make fun of it. They were older, smarter, and stronger than I was.

As time went on, though, I developed a quick wit and thick skin that helped me survive my brothers' bullying. But that experience would lead me to really notice when some classmates were getting made fun of on the school bus. They were quiet or shy, and the older kids took advantage of it. Most days I just kept quiet, thankful that I wasn't the one getting teased.

But one day, on the bus, I couldn't take it anymore. Two eighth-grade boys were making fun of a girl named Danielle. Now, Danielle was a really sweet girl, the kind of girl who would never make fun of someone else. She was smart, soft-spoken, and always nice to people. Danielle was also a beautiful girl with some facial scarring and slight disfigurement from being horribly burned as a young child. On this day, the boys were making fun of her clothes (which didn't make sense since we were all in school uniforms); they were making fun of her hair; and they were making fun of her scars. Just as I was about to say something, we pulled up to the school and everyone exited the bus.

I noticed Danielle trying to fight back tears, but she couldn't. They streamed down her face as she collected her books and bag. That was it.

I leaped off the bus and followed the eighth-grade boys into the school parking lot. I threw down my backpack and unleashed a verbal tirade of anger on them. Kids gathered around. The bus driver quickly exited the bus and tried to calm me down. Teachers came running. Still, I didn't stop. I tore them down the same way they had torn down Danielle. I insulted their looks. I mocked their haircuts. I made fun of their grades, their lack of athletic ability, and their lack of girlfriends. I mocked every level of their personalities until they both were fighting back tears in front of all of their friends. They couldn't even fight back. They were left speechless.

At that moment I felt a hand grab my arm. I swung around, expecting it to be a teacher or, worse yet, one of their friends. Instead, I saw Danielle standing there. "Mark, stop it," she said, "this isn't right."

"Huh?" I thought. Why wasn't she happy? I was defending her and every other student who had been made fun of by these eighth-grade bullies. This wasn't how my "movie moment" was supposed to turn out! Shouldn't I have been lifted up on the shoulders of the other students? No, my story ended with me in the principal's office and half of the eighth-grade students waiting for me at lunchtime.

While I was right in wanting to speak up and defend Danielle's honor, the way I went about it was all wrong. I let my anger get the better of me. I didn't use my head. I didn't act like a Christian in the situation because I didn't pray. I failed to love my enemies. Trying to protect others with no concern for yourself is heroic, indeed, but not if it violates Jesus' commandment to love. Love for God must be primary.

The Bible is filled with heroic people who stood up to bullying, heroic people who loved and saved others through their self-sacrifice. Jesus is the primary example of heroism. A few hundred years before Jesus' birth, however, there lived another hero (a heroine, actually) who is one of the most courageous women in all of Scripture.

She was the Bible's first beauty queen, and her name was Esther.

MORE THAN A PRETTY FACE

Esther was born at a difficult time in Israel's history. You see, long after all the kings, including King David and King Josiah, Jerusalem was destroyed, and most of the Jewish people were deported as slaves to Babylon.

The name *Esther* means "star" in Persian.

Soon after, Babylon was taken over by Persia. The Jewish people were thousands of miles from their home, living under a foreign ruler and being treated as second-class citizens.

This is hard for us in the United States to imagine. We live in a free and powerful country. Even though there is still racial and religious persecution in various parts of the country, most Americans live freely, enjoying basic human rights in a democracy. Imagine, though, living in a culture where you had no rights to speak of and where your race and your religious background left you in danger.

This was the time into which Esther was born. She was an orphan growing up in a foreign land, Persia, and was raised by her distant cousin, Mordecai. Now, Esther was exceptionally beautiful, which was both a blessing and a curse (Esther 2:7).

The Persian queen publicly embarrassed her husband, King Ahasuerus, and as a result, the king began looking for a new bride. Because of Esther's great beauty, she was one of the young women gathered for the king. Esther was **Ahasuerus is the Hebrew form of the Persian name Xerxes.** taken to the palace for preparation and training, with the potential of becoming the next queen of Persia. It was the Bible's own version of a beauty pageant.

Esther caught King Ahasuerus' eye and, eventually, became his new queen. In this culture, however, she was in no way equal to the king. In fact, Queen Esther could only approach the king or enter his court when summoned by him. Any other attempt to approach him was punishable by death. To make matters worse, an incredibly evil man named Haman, who hated the Jewish people, was the prime minister and a high-ranking commander in the king's court.

One day as Haman walked by, Mordecai refused to bow to him, as was prescribed by law. Haman was furious and so he ordered Mordecai to be put to death. But he didn't stop there. Much like Hitler, Haman was a madman bent on the destruction of the Jewish people. He quickly hatched a plan to kill all the Jews by manipulating King Ahasuerus.

Ashes and sackcloth were symbols of mourning and repentance.

When Mordecai learned of the Jewish people's fate, he secretly contacted Queen Esther, asking her to approach the king and to save their people. Queen Esther was now faced with a dilemma: If she approached King Ahasuerus without being summoned, she could be sentenced to death. If she did nothing, her beloved cousin and guardian, Mordecai, would be put to death and the Jewish people would be destroyed.

So Queen Esther prayed. She asked that all of the Jews in the city, Mordecai included, join her in prayer and fasting for her impending visit to the king. Read for yourself about the bravery and holiness of this courageous young woman: Esther 4:1–17.

Catholics wear ashes on Ash Wednesday as an outward sign of our inward repentance.

READ IT: Esther 4:1–17

On the third day of fasting, Queen Esther rose up from the ashes and sackcloth, prepared herself, and entered the court of King Ahasuerus. Each step she took was proof not only of her trust in God but also of her courage and selflessness. In the remaining chapters in the book of Esther, you can (and should) read of Queen Esther's brilliant plot both to save her people and to ensure that Haman would not harm anyone ever again. From her childhood, Mordecai had raised Queen Esther to worship the one true God, not the false gods of the Persians. When it mattered most, it was Esther's intense love for her God and for her people that allowed her to save the day by doing what no one thought possible.

FINDING YOURSELF IN ESTHER'S STORY

- Have you ever been the victim of bullying?
- Have you ever been afraid to speak up, fearing what might happen to you if you do?
- What are some situations, even small ones, in which God is calling you to be more heroic?

We live in a world that is obsessed with outward beauty and physical power. The lesson I learned on the bus that day, however, is the same lesson that Esther learned thousands of years prior: true beauty and true power come from God's Spirit within you.

Esther's outer beauty might have turned heads, but in the end, it was Esther's inner beauty, her love for God and for her people, that saved souls. Danielle's outer beauty may have been "scarred," but in the end, she proved to be the most beautiful person on that bus. She taught me a lot that day about how to love all people, even your enemies.

When we are baptized and confirmed, we receive the power of the Holy Spirit. This might not seem like a big deal to some on earth, but it is a very big deal in heaven. Through the sacraments, God's life (grace) fills you. The Holy Spirit dwells within you and that makes you beautifully dangerous and wonderfully powerful (see Philippians 4:13).

You are not all that different from Esther. You live in a culture where people are constantly being destroyed. You might be destroyed by classmates bullying you at school. You might be destroyed by the pressure to physically measure up to the influencers you see online. You live in a culture where millions of babies have been destroyed through legalized abortion, where people are torn down because of their race, and where countless others are mocked for mental or physical illnesses and diseases that are beyond their control.

Esther was a young woman whom God put in the right place at the right time. God had her right where he wanted her. God has you right where he wants you, too. For others to be saved, Esther had to tap into the Spirit of God within her. And that's what I should have done, too, instead of relying on my own anger and ability to mock the eighth-grade bullies that day at school. Esther had the power. She only had to pray to unleash it. You have the power, too. Are you courageous enough to unleash it? Do you love others enough to put yourself on the line?

There are people, from the unborn to the elderly, who are in need of the love of God working through you. God gave you the Holy Spirit, "a spirit of power and love and self-control" (2 Timothy 1:7). Unleash that power with a loving heart and you, too, will be known throughout heaven and earth for your heroism.

CHAPTER 11

. . . .

Mary: The Bible's First and Perfect Disciple

I hated chores growing up. Vacuuming was a pain. Doing dishes was an annoyance. Folding laundry was no fun. Mowing the grass was miserable. Shoveling snow was even worse. I began looking for the easiest way out of chores. I would eat less, hoping for fewer dishes. I would wear clothes out of my hamper to cut down on laundry. I did my best to cram trash into the container as hard as I could, hoping that by the time it was overflowing it would be my brother's turn to take it out.

I did my chores every week, though, because I was told to do them.

I did them for my allowance. I did them to avoid punishment. But when my mother was pregnant and sick and became unable to take care of us or the house, my motivation changed. I finally did the chores entrusted to me for the right reason: I did them out of love. It didn't mean that the tasks I had to do became more fun or that they didn't include discomfort. After all, yard work is never comfortable, as Adam would tell you (Genesis 3:17–19). It just meant that I endured the discomfort with less whining and with a better attitude because of my love for my parents. Let's be honest, no discomfort I went through could compare to a pregnant woman's, as Eve would tell you (Genesis 3:16).

Since the time of my mother's pregnancy, my attitude toward chores changed for good. I had learned a lesson. As much sacrifice as it took for me to do them, I saw what my mother had gone through to have my little brother. She had sacrificed way more. In fact, my parents had sacrificed many things so that their children could have many things. Chores taught me a lot about discipline and about being part of a family. My parents taught me a lot about self-reliance and hard work through having me do these chores. They also taught me a lot about self-sacrifice and true love by expecting more from me than I was comfortable with giving.

God, too, believes in us more than we believe in ourselves. He knows what we are designed for. He knows all that we are capable of in this life. He knows the necessity of discipline and the importance of obedience. God is a parent who knows that true love is seen in sacrifice. Look at the Cross. That is a Son who lived in loving obedience and a Father who knows about a loving sacrifice. Standing near the Cross, too, was another parent, who understood the love that sacrifice requires and the pain that can come with it.

She was the one soul who was central to Jesus' plan of salvation, a soul that was set apart by God from the beginning so that she could fulfill a unique role. God preserved the Virgin Mary from sin through the Immaculate Conception. He designed Mary for a specific role, the highest privilege given to anyone who has ever lived. Mary became God's perfect dwelling place on earth. This was the vocation she was uniquely suited for, and her yes to God had eternal effects.

JUST AN ORDINARY DAY IN NAZARETH

St. Luke begins the story of the Annunciation by telling us that God sent the angel Gabriel to the town of Nazareth, to a virgin (Luke 1:26–27). The Bible doesn't tell us what the Blessed Virgin Mary was doing at the moment the angel appeared. Tradition tells us that Mary was a teenager, probably about fourteen years old. And since it wasn't the Sabbath (a day set aside when you were not allowed to work), it makes sense to imagine that Mary was probably doing her daily chores.

Life in Galilee was not easy. Men worked hard in their respective trades of fishing, farming, or carpentry (like St. Joseph, who was a carpenter). Women worked equally hard, having to draw water from the well and transport it home, while tending to the children, the house, and the animals, and making meals over a small fire. Children were expected to work hard, too. The "chores" of a child from Jesus' time were more like full-time jobs.

Tradition tells us that Mary's parents were St. Joachim and St. Anne.

Mary was raised by holy parents and knew her Sacred Scripture. She prayed constantly. Her work was a form of prayer. Even as prayerful and as well-versed as she was in the Hebrew Scriptures, she could not have been prepared for an extraordinary encounter with a supernatural visitor.

Picture the scene. Mary is working in the house, possibly on her knees, cleaning or preparing food in the kitchen, when all of a sudden there is a flash of light. She looks up to see a glorious, almost blinding presence.

Imagine the room. Envision the angel. Close your eyes and really see our Mother Mary and the angel Gabriel. Now, slowly read Luke 1:26–38 and pay attention to the details of the story.

READ IT: Luke 1:26–38

The archangel's first word to Mary is "Hail!" Now, this doesn't mean, "What's up?" or, "How ya' doing?" No, the Greek word for "Hail!" means "Rejoice!"

The news that the angel brought was not only good news, it was great news! Mary had a reason to rejoice and so do we. God's mission to save us was kicking into high gear, and that rescue mission was going to occur through a fourteen-year-old virgin from a tiny, rural town.

The angel then said a phrase that had never been uttered before, proclaiming Mary to be "full of grace" (Luke 1:28). Nowhere in the Old Testament had anyone ever been addressed like this. In fact, this is the only time in the Bible that an angel addresses someone with a title and not just their name. Grace can best be described as "God's life in us." Mary was so filled with God's life from the beginning, even before this en-

Ave Maria is Latin for "Hail Mary!"

counter, that she was the only one worthy of such a title. Also, Gabriel's proclamation of "the Lord is with you" must have been comforting to Mary since a life-changing meeting with an angel probably wasn't on her list of chores for that day.

As Gabriel went on to share the great news about God's Son taking flesh in her womb, he reminded her not to fear. Throughout the Bible, when the Creator draws near to his creation, he must calm our hearts and remind us not to fear him. Mary was no different. She wasn't so much scared as she was overcome with awe and overwhelmed with a question.

The Blessed Virgin Mary is "immaculate," which comes from the Latin for "unstained" or "sinless."

"And Mary said to the angel, 'How shall this be, since I have no husband?'" (Luke 1:34).

Twice before, we are told that Mary is a virgin (Luke 1:27). So, Mary's question, "How can this be, since I have no husband?" is more about her being a virgin than it is about being unmarried, though she was already betrothed, or promised, to St. Joseph (Luke 1:34). Mary didn't doubt God's ability or promise; she was trying to figure out how it was going to work.

Thanks to the overabundance of grace that God granted to Mary from the moment of her own Immaculate Conception, she was absolutely capable of the mission she was about to undertake.

Mary's last words to the angel were the most beautiful words ever uttered by any teenager in history: "Behold, I am the handmaid of the Lord; let it be to me according to your word" (Luke 1:38).

In that one line, Mary proclaimed it all. God comes

first. We are his servants, and she was his handmaid. What God wants comes first. God's plan for Mary came first. She trusted him completely. She trusted his plan wholeheartedly. She didn't know what would come next. She wasn't sure how it was all going to work. She just knew that she was filled with God's life and that she shouldn't fear because God had a plan! So she said yes with every part of her soul and changed history forever. Mary turned in her teenage duties to become the Mother of God.

FINDING YOURSELF IN MARY'S STORY

- Have you ever felt like God expected too much from you?
- Are you afraid that God's calling for you might include suffering?
- Do you rejoice each day that God knows you and loves you?
- Do you trust God enough to let him be in complete control of your life?

It might be difficult for you to compare your life to Mary's life. She was a pregnant virgin at fourteen. She had to tell her fiancé that God was the father of her child. She had to travel almost one hundred miles in her third trimester of pregnancy and give birth in the filthiest of settings. After Jesus' birth, a prophet told Mary that she was going to suffer tremendously. She had random wise men from thousands of miles away show up with gifts, wanting to worship her baby boy. Then, Mary, Joseph, and Jesus had to escape to a foreign country when the king went on a murdering rampage, looking for her newborn son.

Mary is different. She's unique in every way. She is God's own Mother. She is a virgin, pure and sinless, and the perfect model of chastity. She is filled with God's life (grace) and is a part of God's salvation plan for us all. Oh, and one more thing, Mary is not just Jesus' mother, she's your mother, too (John 19:27). It might seem like Mary is as far from you as you are from heaven, but that's not entirely true. Through the sacraments, specifically the Eucharist, we are also filled with God's grace. God has a plan for you. Your life will play a role in the salvation of others. Your life will have suffering. And your life will have incredible joy if you know Christ intimately and follow God daily, as Mary did.

The Lord is with you.

That's right, the Lord wasn't just with Mary. He is with you! He is with you in the sacraments, in his Word, in the priesthood, in the Church. The Holy Spirit is God, and the Holy Spirit lives within you. So you, not unlike Mary, are filled with God's grace. And also, like Mary, God has a plan for your life. His plan will include suffering at times, but it is in those times that we need to lean into the grace that God offers us and remember the words that Mary heard on that incredible day: "Do not be afraid."

Do not be afraid. Suffering doesn't mean that God doesn't love you. Trust in God's grace. Lean into that grace and you can get through any situation (Philippians 4:13). God is going to put some situations in your path to help you grow in holiness and to help others experience his love. These situations might feel like chores some days. From time to time, they might even feel like obstacles in

> **The Rosary helps us focus on Jesus' life through the eyes and heart of Mary.**

your life. You can reject them and run from them. You can get through them, but with a bad attitude. Or you can embrace them and trust in the Lord's plans.

Mary's love for the Father allowed her to fulfill her vocation with joy and with grace. It wasn't easy, but it wasn't a chore. The more you seek to love your Heavenly Father and to live a life like Mary's, the more fulfilling your life will become and the less your tasks will feel like chores.

Life is only a chore if you let it be. Life can also be an adventure if you just "let it be [done] ... according to [God's] word."

CHAPTER 12

. . . .

The "Loaves and Fish" Kid: The Bible's First Busboy

At age ten, I decided I wanted to make some money. My allowance just wasn't cutting it. There were skateboard parts to buy and video games to master, and so I told my parents I needed a higher allowance. They told me to get a job. Over the next few years, I delivered thousands of newspapers. I delivered over two hundred papers a day. Long before people got their news online, I was their search engine. I had a spotless record and a growing bank account. I took pride in my work. Once high school started, though, I had to find a different job, one that worked with my schedules for school, sports, and band.

I had tasted freedom with my own stream of income, and I didn't want to live without it. I soon traded in newspapers for a spot-ridden apron and tray. I took a job as a lowly busboy in a nearby restaurant. I never understood why they called the job "busboy." Later, though, I learned that the word "busboy" comes from the Latin word *omnibus*, which means "for all." It was applied to busboys because it is their job to do "anything and everything for anyone and everyone" in the restaurant. Truthfully, that's how it was.

I did everything. I set the tables, delivered food, cleared plates, restocked food, wiped down tables, swept, and vacuumed. You name it, I did it. Customers didn't know my name. Customers didn't know how hard I was working behind the scenes or how badly I needed money, especially since I was saving for college. The only things that mattered to them were that their water glasses were always full, their baskets of chips overflowing, and the salsa endlessly flowing like a waterfall of spicy goodness. I was on the main stage every night, but somehow I remained almost anonymous and behind the scenes. Thanks in part to my unsung efforts, people left that restaurant more stuffed than the enchiladas. Each night, the waiters may have left with far more money in their pockets, but I fell into bed with the great satisfaction of knowing I had gone above and beyond the call of duty.

St. Martha is the patron saint of waiters and waitresses. You might remember how she waited on and served the Lord (Luke 10:38–42). However, there is no official patron saint designated specifically for bussers, which got me to thinking. I'd like to suggest one character, in particular, who I think would make a great patron saint of busboys.

THE LUNCH RUSH
BY THE SEA OF GALILEE

Jesus performed countless miracles during his time on earth. We are blessed that many of them were written down in the Gospels. One of the miracles that appears in all four Gospel accounts, and one of the most famous miracles of all time, is the multiplication of the loaves and the fish. You have probably heard this story more times than you can count. Sometimes it's important to read it again, however, with your own eyes. Oftentimes when you look at it on your own, rather than having others read it to you, you'll pick up on little details you might have missed in the past.

Read John 6:1–14 and pay attention to the details.

READ IT: John 6:1–14

OK, now answer the following questions:

Where did this take place, next to what famous

site? When did this take place, during what feast? How much money would still not be enough to feed everyone? Who tells Jesus about the boy with the food? How much food does the boy have? What kind of bread was it? How many men were there, not counting the women and children? What, specifically, did Jesus do with the bread and fish? How much food was left over after Jesus' miracle?

Did you catch any details you had forgotten? Did you notice anything new?

Over the years, I've heard a lot of priests and speakers talk about the boy with the loaves and the fish. They always praised his generosity and affirmed his sacrifice. While I don't want to disagree, because the boy does deserve our admiration, the homilies and talks always annoy me a little.

First, I have never liked the fact that the kid didn't have a name. I mean, of course he had a name, but the Gospel writers don't tell us what it is, which bothers me. If this kid is so important, why didn't someone stop to ask his name? I think we should call him Billy. Billy sounds like a good guy. Billy's the kind of kid who'll share his lunch with you at school when you accidentally leave

Some scholars believe that the "loaves" were probably more the size of buns.

yours on the counter. Yep, I vote that from here on out, or at least in this book, we officially refer to "the loaves and fish kid" as Billy.

Scripture should capture our imagination and cause us to think. When you're reading a story, don't just ask, "What is this saying to me?" Really put yourself into the scene, into each character's sandals, and ask, "What is this saying *about* me?"

The Sea of Galilee is approximately thirteen miles long and five miles wide. It is a very important site in the Gospels.

Billy didn't set out to be a hero. We don't even know what he was doing there that day. Maybe he just noticed the crowd while walking by the Sea of Galilee and decided to investigate. Maybe, like David, he was just delivering lunch to someone in his family when he found himself in an awkward situation.

Possibly, the most important part of Billy's story isn't what he did, but why he did it. What did he hear in the Apostles' voices? What did he see in Jesus' eyes? He was most likely from a poor family. He probably fit right in with the masses of people who came to Jesus hungry. Only this day, for some reason, Billy had some food. He didn't know what Christ was going to do, but he gave the Lord all that he had. Christ honored Billy's sacrifice, blessings thousands of people through it.

All Billy did was give back to God what he had already been given. That food, while it was technically Billy's, was really God's. Every gift you have is a gift from God. Everything you have, even those things you buy with your own money, is a gift from God. Billy didn't withhold creation (loaves and fish) from his Creator, and as a result, even more of God's creation—literally thousands of people—were blessed by it.

Barley was considered "poor peoples' food." Since the boy was not wealthy, his sacrifice is that much more powerful.

Never underestimate how much God can do with a little. Never underestimate how much God can do with you, an ordinary person, on an ordinary day.

FINDING YOURSELF IN "BILLY'S" STORY

- Have you ever given everything you had to the Lord?

- Do you give your absolute best to everything you do?
- Is it more desirable for you to be famous or to be faithful? To be rich or to be holy?
- Do you think Billy would care that his name isn't listed in the Gospel accounts? Or do you think he was so overwhelmed with what he witnessed that his own glory was the furthest thing from his mind?

He witnessed a miracle of love. He witnessed God in action. The God of the universe thought enough of Billy to invite him to play a major role in one of the most famous and miraculous moments in history. He looked Love in the eyes and watched how Love magnified his little act of love. Billy's life was instantly changed, forever.

Just think about how many people benefited from Billy's charity, and not just the thousands on the shore of the sea. Billions of souls have read and heard this true story, having their lives both challenged and blessed by it.

For a nameless kid, he made quite a name for himself. How about you?

Do you worry that your best just isn't good enough? You have more to offer than you think. When you give God your everything, he can do amazing things. God can do miraculous things with what you offer back to him.

The first thing you have to do is remember where your gifts, talents, and blessings come from. They are all gifts from God. When you put them back into his hands, for his use and for his glory, he can and will do incredible things—not only in your life, but also in the lives of countless other people. You are powerful beyond your wildest dreams. Did you know that? There is power in sacrifice. Just as Jesus did with Billy, God can unleash that power. When you put your gifts in his hands, he multiplies them!

Pour your best into everything you do. Take pride in your schoolwork. Take responsibility around the house. Make your room the kind of place that would make your parents proud. Whatever it is that you like to do, whether it's sports, dance, music, or writing, do it well. Give it your best, because the God who gave you that talent deserves your best at all times (Colossians 3:15–17).

After Jesus' miracle with the loaves and fish, he goes on to explain a greater miracle with bread: the Eucharist (John 6:22–71).

You don't have to be all things to all people, but

you're invited to be the absolute best version of yourself that you can be, every hour of the day. And you can do that by putting others first, by serving them just like Jesus did (John 13:15). If you live this way, you won't be bussing the banquet table in heaven. You'll be sitting as the guest of honor, right beside Jesus, enjoying the fruits of a job well done and a life well lived.

CHAPTER 13

· ·

Timothy: The Bible's Last Apprentice

When people ask you, "What are you going to be when you grow up?" how do you respond? What are your dreams for your future? Have they changed at all? Oftentimes when we think about our future job, we try to envision ourselves in settings that we think would make us happy. At the same time, we also try to eliminate certain jobs based on things we dislike.

For example, if you dislike blood, you will probably cross doctor or paramedic off your potential job list. If you have a fear of heights, you probably won't apply to be a skydiving instructor or a window washer. If you don't love math, you might want to avoid accounting. If you don't like getting dirty, you probably won't enjoy plumbing or farming. And if you lack patience, teaching is probably not for you.

Some people pick jobs for the power, others for the hours, and many for the money. Some people just take whatever they can get and wait until something better comes along. Work is work. There are bills to pay and food to buy. A job is a job, right?

Well, yes and no.

Where does God fit into all this? At what point do you stop and really pray to God, asking him to guide you into your future, not only including your job, but also your vocation? Do you pray about whether you are called to be married or single, a priest or religious sister or brother?

Your parents might also have a plan for you. You might have the "perfect" plan for your own life. As well-intentioned and perfect as your plans or your parents' plans are, they are nowhere near as perfect as God's plan for you.

Timothy was likely born in Lystra (modern-day Turkey).

In fact, read Jeremiah 29:11–12. Commit it to memory. It's one of the most important verses you can pray as you consider your future. God has a plan for your life, one that only you can fulfill. It begins with you trusting him and saying yes.

St. Paul had a plan for his life. God had another.

St. Paul started out merely as Saul, a very

intelligent and well-respected man, with a strong hatred for Christians. Saul changed his mind, however, after the Lord spoke to his heart. Saul went from despising those who followed Jesus to giving his very life so that everyone in the world would know of Christ's love. Saul became St. Paul,

Timothy means "honored by God."

the world's greatest missionary and the writer of almost half of the New Testament. He didn't know where God was going to lead him from day to day, or from year to year. St. Paul was constantly praying, asking the Holy Spirit to guide and direct his path (Acts 16:6).

St. Paul met an array of interesting people on his travels around the Mediterranean world. Some were friendly. Many were not. During his first missionary journey, St. Paul, along with St. Barnabas, ended up in an area called Galatia, located in modern-day Turkey. There, in the cities of Derbe and Lystra, they preached the Gospel message in the marketplace each day. It was there that a young man named Timothy, probably a teenager, first heard the Good News of Jesus Christ from his future mentor and friend, St. Paul.

Timothy's story picks up several years later. When St. Paul and his new traveling companion, Silas, come back through Galatia on another missionary journey, Timothy, now a young adult, catches their attention.

TINY TIM GROWS INTO ST. TIMOTHY

The Acts of the Apostles tells us that Timothy was the son of a Jewish mother and a Greek father. He must have learned about the faith and about the Hebrew Scriptures from his mother, Lois, and his grandmother, Eunice (2 Timothy 1:5). He was apparently a very well-respected young man in his community, and the leaders there spoke so highly of him that St. Paul invited Timothy along on his missionary work (Acts 16:1–2).

The rest of what we know about St. Timothy we learn from the rest of St. Paul's letters, which are called epistles. Over the next fifteen to twenty years, St. Timothy would see a whole new world. God sent Timothy into situations the young disciple never would have chosen on his own.

Timothy traveled with Paul to Philippi and began to watch over the newly formed Church there. Later, Timothy would travel to Thessalonica, preaching and teaching the Gospel. Timothy was with Paul as he wrote his letters to the good people of Thessalonica (1 and 2 Thessalonians) and traveled to Ephesus and back through Greece. In addition to other travels, Timothy would be with Paul during his imprisonment in Rome and, eventually,

St. Paul commends Timothy for his loyalty in Philippians 2:19.

would be left in Ephesus as a leader, to deal with problems that were erupting there (1 Timothy 1:3–4).

There are two letters to Timothy in the New Testament and both are attributed to St. Paul. When you read them, you can see the love and friendship that the two great evangelists shared. St. Paul respected St. Timothy very much and spoke highly of him (Philippians 2:19–22).

Timothy boldly confronted false teachers (1 Timothy 1:3).

Timothy must have been feeling overwhelmed by his position in Ephesus. It's tough enough being a young leader, teaching about God and his Word to people twice your age. St. Paul's letters are written to strengthen and encourage St. Timothy. There were many false teachers and inappropriate practices going on in Ephesus, which were challenging for St. Timothy.

Take a few minutes and read 1 Timothy 4:6–16 and 2 Timothy 4:1–6.

READ IT: 1 Timothy 4:6–16 and 2 Timothy 4:1–6

In St. Paul, Timothy had more than a good friend or traveling companion. St. Paul was Timothy's mentor and teacher. This makes St. Timothy one of the Bible's last known apprentices, and a true gift to the early Church. Tradition tells us that St. Timothy continued ministering in Ephesus and was eventually martyred for the Faith around the year AD 95.

Growing up in Lystra, St. Timothy probably had different plans for his life. No young boy's dream is to be chased out of towns, mocked, and eventually martyred for the Faith. At the same time, St. Timothy also knew a deeper joy that many never experience: the joy of knowing Jesus Christ intimately and sharing in his life and grace on a daily basis. St. Timothy saw the world.

1 Timothy 4:12 is one of the most famous "teen" verses in the Bible.

St. Timothy witnessed miracles. St. Timothy humbly spoke with authority and power as he served Jesus Christ and his Church. Through St. Timothy's yes to God, countless souls came to know God and were saved. Today, over 2,000 years later, we honor St. Timothy as one of the great early saints of our Church.

FINDING YOURSELF IN TIMOTHY'S STORY

- Are you willing to do what God calls you to do and to go where God calls you to go?
- Are you open to whatever vocation, even priesthood or religious life, that God calls you to?
- Are you willing to be uncomfortable or to suffer for your Faith?
- Do you doubt yourself? Do you doubt God's presence within you?

You are a work of art, unique and beautiful and amazing. You are a complete one-of-a-kind masterpiece, created and handcrafted by a Creator. You are designed to reflect the light of Christ to all whom you encounter.

These are all true statements, whether or not you agree with them. Do you believe these statements? Do you feel this way about yourself? Do you feel unique and beautiful? Do you believe you are the handiwork of God, created and designed with purpose and dignity? Do you believe you glorify him and reflect his light to the world?

If not, it might be a sign that you need to pray more, to read more Sacred Scripture and to start seeing yourself as God sees you, rather than how you have begun to see yourself. If not, it might be time to head to the

Sacrament of Reconciliation and get rid of the blinders we call sin.

Read and pray these Scripture passages:

READ IT:
- **Psalm 139:14–16**
- **Matthew 10:30**
- **Ephesians 2:10**
- **Genesis 1:26–27**
- **Isaiah 41:10**

God believes in you so strongly that he doesn't leave you alone. God sends you people in your life to offer you good examples. Hopefully, they're in your own home. Hopefully, there are holy and joyful people in your parish and your school. God will send you who you need, just as he did for Timothy.

Timothy's mother taught him the Jewish faith, while his father, a Greek, could not. God didn't leave Timothy spiritually orphaned, though. He sent him St. Paul to be his mentor, guide, and spiritual foster father. God provided for young Timothy so he could fulfill the role and vocation that God had designed for him. God will do the same for you. God believes in you more than you believe in yourself.

Live like Timothy …

Be open. Stay humble. Follow holy people. Ask questions. Keep learning. Be courageous. Never stop praying. Live. Love.

St. Timothy knew how to love people, and it is love, not just knowledge of the Faith, that wins hearts for Jesus Christ. If the person you are talking to doesn't believe that you love them, it doesn't matter how smart you are when you speak to them. Love changes lives. Love heals wounds. Love saves souls.

God believes in you. I believe in you, too.

The question is not whether God will send you a mentor. God will send people, holy people, to lead you. The question is: Will you follow?

CONCLUSION

· · · · · · · · · · · · · · · · · · · ·

OK, so if you are reading this, you are amazing. You are epic. You have now taken a deep dive into the Bible in a way that most adults haven't ever done. Well done!

Hopefully along the way you learned a few things, not only about how God thinks and acts and "works," but also about how much you have in common with young men and women who lived thousands of years ago. Aside from technology, not a lot has really changed, right? We all still have the same desires, the same struggles, the same temptations ... and, if you trust, the same happy endings to most of the challenging situations in life.

So, what now?

Will this just be a "nice book I read about Biblical characters" or will this be a turning point in your life? Will you, like the characters you have read about in these pages, allow the Holy Spirit to change and transform your life into something amazing, or will you just go through the motions each day like so many of your peers?

God made you unique.

God designed you for a purpose.

God has blessed you beyond your understanding.

God desires to use you to lead others to him.

Will you say yes?

Consider the characters you just read about. None of them could control their life. None of them fully understood all that God was calling them to do or be. They just trusted. They woke up each day and prayed. They sought the Lord daily and trusted that if they stayed connected to him, things would work out ... and they did.

Your story will not be recorded on the pages of Sacred Scripture, but your story can still change peoples' lives for the better. Your example can lead your family and friends and even your enemies closer to God.

The question you need to answer is whether you will allow the Lord to change you. Will you let the Holy Spirit unleash the hidden excellence within you? Will you let God make you a saint?

Now, before you say that idea seems unreachable, you'll need to read more about the saints (and that's a different book altogether). God made saints out of far, far "worse" people than you. Take the heroes in this book as proof that God can work with all different types of people.

God is within you. He loves you. He is proud of you, and he wants to use you to do great things in this world, just like he did with these young men and women.

All you have to do is *let him*.